IRISH COMPANY LAW INDEX

by

DONAL McGAHON

GILL AND MACMILLAN

Published in Ireland by
Gill and Macmillan Ltd
Goldenbridge
Dublin 8
with associated companies in
Auckland, Delhi, Gaborone, Hamburg, Harare,
Hong Kong, Johannesburg, Kuala Lumpur, Lagos, London,
Manzini, Melbourne, Mexico City, Nairobi,
New York, Singapore, Tokyo

Print origination by Seton Music Graphics, Co. Cork and
Billing and Sons Ltd, Worcester

British Library Cataloguing in Publication Data
McGahon, Donal
Irish Company Law Index
I.
Title
ISBN 0 7171 1816 9 paperback

To my beloved wife Margaret

CONTENTS

Introduction	
Abbreviations, Terms Used, and References	
Index	1
Index to Table A, Companies Act, 1963 (as amended)	151
Schedule of Forms	168
Schedule of Orders	175
Table of Offences and Penalties	182

INTRODUCTION

This is an index to the provisions of the Companies Acts, 1963 to 1990. The full titles of these Acts are set out in the following page.

There are approximately 400 main headings and 3,000 sub-headings. Cross references are given where relevant or helpful.

The Index includes references to Statutory Instruments and such other Acts which affect the Companies Acts.

A simple numbering system is used to refer to the Acts and Orders. This is given in the following page.

The Companies Act, 1990 is being brought into force by a series of Ministerial Orders. Those made up to the time of going to press are included but readers should obtain details of any subsequent Orders.

The book contains the law up to 11 March 1991.

Suggestions and corrections for future editions will be very welcome.

ABBREVIATIONS, TERMS USED AND REFERENCES

The legislation under which Irish companies operate is set out in Acts and Orders of the Oireachtas. These are referred to as follows :

Reference	**Act**
63/	Companies Act, 1963
77/	Companies (Amendment) Act, 1977
78/	Mergers, Takeovers & Monopolies (Control) Act,1978
82/	Companies (Amendment) Act, 1982
83/	Companies (Amendment) Act, 1983
86/	Companies (Amendment) Act, 1986
90/	Companies (Amendment) Act, 1990
90B/	Companies Act, 1990
ST63/	Stock Transfer Act, 1963
	Orders
1964/41	Companies Act 1963 (Commencement) Order, 1964
1964/42	Companies (Recognition of Countries) Order,1964
1964/43	Companies (Stock Exchange) Order,1964
1964/44	Companies (Fees) Order, 1964
1964/45	Companies (Forms) Order, 1964
1975/198	Companies (Stock Exchange) Order, 1975
1976/64	Companies (Fees) Order, 1976
1978/95	Companies (Amendment) Act 1977 (Commencement) Order, 1978
1979/122	Companies (Amendment) Act 1977 (Designation of Stock Exchange (Nominee) Regulations, 1979
1980/400	Companies (Fees) Order, 1980
1982/25	Companies (Amendment) Act 1982 (Commencement) Order, 1982

Reference	Orders
1982/256	Companies (Forms) Order, 1982
1983/259	Companies (Fees) Order, 1983
1983/288	Companies (Amendment) Act 1983 (Commencement) Order, 1983
1983/289	Companies (Forms) Order, 1983
1987/99	Companies (Fees) Order, 1987
1987/147	Companies (Forms) Order, 1987
1988/54	Companies (Amendment) Act, 1982 (Section 13(2)) Order, 1988
1990/224	Companies (Forms) Order, 1990
1990/336	Companies Act, 1990 (Commencement) Order,1990
1990/337	Companies (Stock Exchange) Regulations, 1990
1991/10	Companies Act, 1990 (Commencement) Order, 1991
1973/163	European Communities (Companies) Regulations, 1973
1984/282	European Communities (Stock Exchange) Regulations, 1984
1987/137	European Communities (Mergers and Divisions of Companies) Regulations, 1987
1989/78	European Communities (Undertakings for Collective Investment in Transferable Securities) Regulations, 1989
1991/18	European Communities (Stock Exchange) (Amendment) Regulations, 1991
Rules	Rules of the Superior Courts

Schedules in the Acts are shown by Roman Numerals, e.g. paragraph 30 of the Third Schedule of the Companies Act, 1963 would be shown as 63/III/30

(Abbreviations: "S" = Schedule, "p" = Part, "Or" = Order, "r" = rule)

ACCOUNT, BOOKS OF

auditors' duty with respect to, 90B/194
basis has to be continuous and consistent, 90B/202(2)
computer, on, power to keep, 77/4
content, 90B/202 (63/147-AM 82/I repealed 90B/6), 63/VI-AM 90B/231(2)
duty of company to keep, 90B/202 (63/147-AM 82/I repealed by 90B/6)
liability of officers where proper books not kept, 90B/203-204
matters relating to, 90B/202 (63/147 repealed by 90B/6)
penalties for failure, 90B/202 (63/147-AM 82/I repealed by 90B/6), 90B/203 (63/296 repealed by 90B/6)
place to be kept at, 90B/202 (63/147-AM 82/I repealed by 90B/6)
preservation of, 90B/202 (63/147 repealed by 90B/6)

ACCOUNTANTS

what, may make report to be set out in prospectus, 63/IIIpIII/30

ACCOUNTS

[see **Auditors' report; Balance sheet; Directors' report; Notes to the accounts; Profit and loss account**]
"abbreviated accounts", publication, 86/19
Act of 1986, exemptions from, 86/2
alteration of Companies Acts' requirements relating to, power of Minister, 63/395 & 396
annual general meeting, and, 63/148-AM 82/I, see 86/3, 83/49, see 90B/260(2)
assurance company of, 63/VIpIII, see 83/9(13b) & 90B/193

continued

Accounts continued
auditors, rights and duties of in connection with, 90B/193 (63/163 repealed by 90B/6), see 83/49(3b)
balance sheet, [see **Balance sheet**]
banking or discount company, of, 63/VIpIII, see 83/9(13b)
books of, [see **Account, books of**]
books of, form of, 63/378-AM 77/4-AM 82/I
-how and where to be kept, 90B/202 (63/147-AM 82/I repealed by 90B/6), see 86/S28(3)
-proper not kept, or deemed to be kept, liability when, 90B/203 (63/296-AM 82/I repealed by 90B/6)
"called up share capital", 86/S notes to balance sheet 9
"capitalisation", 86/S62
companies liquidation, [see **Companies Liquidation Account**]
comparative figures to be shown, 86/4(8), S44
contents and form of, 63/149, 63/VI-AM 90B/231(2), see 83/9(12) & 9(13a) & 49 & 86/3
defective, liability of directors for, 63/149(7)-AM 82/I, 63/150(4)-AM 82/I, see 86/S76
delivery to registrar, 86/7 & 18
directors, particulars of salaries and pensions in, 63/191(1), see 86/S49
documents annexed to accounts, 63/164
duty to prepare, lay and deliver, 63/148, see 86/3, 86/7 & 18
exemptions for small and medium-sized companies, 86/10-I2
express requirements to keep, 90B/202 (63/147-AM 82/I repealed by 90B/6)
foreign company of, provisions as to, 63/354
form and content, 86/3 & S
group, [see **Group accounts**]
"historical cost accounting rules", 86/S17 & 65
holding and subsidiary companies of, 63/VIpII, 86/S45-55
holding company, duty to prepare etc., 63/150, see 86/S76 & 90B/41 & 43
holding company, statement about subsidiaries, 63/151
interpretation and provisions of Schedule, 86/S60-75
continued

Accounts continued
investment companies, special provisions for, 86/3 & S56-59
investments, 86/S31 & 66
"liability", 86/S70
liability where not properly kept, 90B/203 (63/296-AM 82/I repealed by 90B/6)
liquidator, of
-in creditors' voluntary winding up, 63/272-AM 82/I-AM 90B/145, 63/273-AM 82/I, see 82/16
-in members' voluntary winding up, 63/262-AM 82/I-AM 90B/145, 63/263-AM 82/I, see 82/16
"loans", 86/S67
loans to directors, particulars of, to be shown in, 90B/41-45 (63/192 cesser 90B/49), see 86/S49
materiality, power to disregard immaterial amounts in particular cases, 86/S68
meaning of, 63/2(1)
medium-sized companies, exemption for, 86/11 & 12
-reclassification, 86/9
members and debenture holders entitled to, 63/159-AM 82/I
Minister may alter, 63/395(1), 86/24
- certain classes of company exempted, 63/VIpIII, see 83/9(13b) & 90B/193
modification for small or medium-sized companies, 86/10-12
particulars of directors' salaries and other payments to be annexed to, 63/191, see 86/S49
particulars to be given by directors, and, 63/193-AM 90B/53(11)
preparation, duty of directors, 63/148
profit and loss, 63/157-AM 82/I, see 83/9(13a) & 83/49, & 86/18
provisions as to, 63/VI, see 83/9(12) & 45 & 47 & 49
provisions, 86/S69 & 70
publication, 86/19
"purchase price", 86/S71
"realised profits", 86/S72

continued

Accounts continued
receiver, to be furnished by, 63/319(1) & (2), 63/321-AM 82/I-AM 90B/145, see 82/16
-enforcement of duty to deliver, 63/322
"related companies", 86/S73
signed by two directors, 63/156(1)-AM 82/I
small company, exemptions for, 86/10 & 12
-reclassification, 86/9
staff costs, 86/S74
staff, particulars of, 86/S42
stock-in-trade, 86/S13 & 15 & 19
transactions involving directors and others, disclosure, 90B/41
translation of, 63/128(1)
"turnover", 86/S75
unregistered company, application of provisions to, 63/377-AM 90B/250, 90B/250 (replacing 86/21), see 1987/137

ACQUISITION BY COMPANY OF ITS OWN SHARES

general prohibition, 83/41, see 1987/137 & 1989/78 & 90B/260(2)
nominee of company, acquisition by, 83/42
otherwise than for valuable consideration, 83/41(2), see 1987/137 & 1989/78
treatment of own shares acquired by public limited company, 83/43-AM 90B/232
[see **Financial assistance by Company for Acquisition of its shares; Purchase by Company of its own shares**]

ACQUISITION OF OWN SHARES AND SHARES IN HOLDING COMPANY

"distribution", 90B/206
documents, retention and inspection of, 90B/222
insiders, unlawful dealings by, 90B/223
Minister may make regulations as to, 90B/228
offences, 90B/234

continued

Acquisition of own shares and shares in holding company continued
own shares
-assignment or release of company's right to purchase, 90B/217
-contingent purchase contracts, 90B/214
-duration of authority granted by public limited company to purchase, 90B/216
-effect of company's failure to purchase, 90B/219
-incidental payments, 90B/218
-market purchases, 90B/212
.authority for, 90B/215
-power of company to purchase, 90B/211
.not permitted if the nominal value of non-redeemable issued share capital is less than ten per cent of total issued share capital, 90B/211(3)
-off-market purchases, 90B/212
.authority for, 90B/213
recognised stock exchange
-company's duty to inform about purchase, 90B/229
-duty in relation to unlawful purchases, 90B/230
redeemable shares
-construction of references to redeemable preference shares, 90B/221
-definition, 90B/206
-power to convert shares into, 90B/210
.not permitted if the nominal value of non-redeemable issued share capital is less than ten per cent of total issued share capital, 90B/210(4)
-power to issue, 90B/207
.not permitted if the nominal value of non-redeemable issued share capital is less than ten per cent of total issued share capital, 90B/207(2)
-redemption of existing redeemable preference shares, 90B/220
redemption
-cancellation of shares on, 90B/208
-effect of company's failure to do so, 90B/219
-existing redeemable preference shares, of, 90B/220
continued

Acquisition of own shares and shares in holding company continued
.not permitted if the nominal value of non-redeemable issued share capital is less than ten per cent of total issued share capital, 90B/207(2)
-companies capital duty relief on re-issue of shares, 90B/208(c)
registrar, returns to be made to, 90B/226
subsidiary holding shares in its holding company, 90B/224
-civil liability for improper purchase, 90B/225
treasury shares, 90B/209
-nominal value must not exceed ten per cent of issued share capital, 90B/209(2)

ACQUISITION OF SHARES OF DISSENTIENTS

provisions as to, 63/204, see 1987/137

ACTIONS

[see **Proceedings**]

ACTS

amendments of other, 63/399, 63/XI
enactments repealed, 63/XII
joint stock banks, relating to, provisions of, not repealed, 63/3, 63/XIII
provisions of certain, unaffected by Act, 63/377(2)
public general statute, body incorporated under, 63/377(2)
reference in, to companies registered under 1908 Act, 63/4
repeal of and savings, 63/3
and, 63/XII, 63/XIII [see **Companies Acts**]
Trade Union Act 1871, not affected, 63/3

ADJOURNED MEETING

resolution passed at, date of, 63/144, see 90/23(6), 63/266(5), 63/308

AFFIDAVIT

verifying statement of affairs, in winding up by the
court or where provisional liquidator appointed,
63/224-AM 82/I, see 90B/18
-submitted to receiver, 63/320-AM 82/I-AM 90B/173,
see 82/16

AGENT

acquisition or disposal of interest in shares, by
[see **Disclosure of interests in shares of public limited company**]
counsel not included in expression, 63/2(1)
duties of, in connection with investigations, 90B/7-23
(replacing 63/168-AM 82/7)
examiner as, 90/7(7)
liability of, for pre-formation contracts, 63/37
liability of, where keeping register or index of
members, 63/120
meaning of, 63/2(1)

AIRCRAFT

charge on, or share of, requires registration, 63/99-AM
90B/122

ALLOTMENT OF SHARES

[see **Offer of shares or debentures to public; Prospectus; Share capital**]
cash, for, meaning, 83/2(3)
consideration other than cash, for, meaning, 83/2(3)
delivery of return to registrar within one month,
63/58-AM 82/I, see 83/31(2) & 55(1g) & 1987/137
directors, by,
-authority by special resolution, 83/20
-authority required for, 83/20
.relief from compliance with rules, 83/20
.renewal of, 83/20

continued

Allotment of shares continued
-general authority for, 83/20
-offence in relation to, 83/20(7)
discount, at, prohibition, 83/27
irregular, consequence of, 63/57-AM 82/I
maximum amount, to be stated in authorisation, 83/20(3)
minimum subscription, and, 63/53-AM 83/I, 83/22
offer for sale to public with view to, 63/51, see 82/21(2)
partial subscription, statement in prospectus
regarding, 83/22
payment for, 83/28
personal liability of director, and, 63/53
private company, prohibition of allotment with a view
to offer for sale to public, 83/21
prohibited in certain cases, unless statement in lieu of
prospectus delivered, 63/54-AM 82/I-AM 83/I
prospectus issued generally, in pursuance of,
63/56-AM 82/I
public limited company, by, additional restrictions on,
63/53-AM 83/I, see 83/22, 63/56, 63/57
relevant securities, for which authorisation required,
83/23, see 1989/78
rights of pre-emption in, 83/23, see 1989/78 & 90B/260(2)
share capital, of, when not to be made unless minimum
subscription received, 63/53-AM 83/I, see 83/22(2)
specified conditions relating to, 63/53
stock exchange nominee, to, 77/2
stock exchange quotation, and, 63/57
subscriber of memorandum, and, 63/31(1), 83/35
term of effect of authorisation, 83/20
time elapsing between issue of prospectus and, 63/56
time for, after prospectus issued, 63/56
voidable by applicant, when, 63/55-AM 83/I, see 83/22(2)
-in cases where prospectus states application has been
or will be made for shares to be dealt in on Stock
Exchange, when, 63/57-AM 82/I
when paid for, 83/2(2)

ALTERNATIVE ACCOUNTING RULES

application to company accounts, 86/S17-22
current cost, rules for inclusion of assets at, 86/S19
depreciation rules and, 86/S20
revaluation reserve, 86/S22

ALTERNATIVE REMEDY

oppression, in case of, 63/205, see 90/5(4)
petition grounded on affidavit, Rules

AMALGAMATION

compensation for loss of office on, 63/187, 63/188
compromise or arrangement involving, 63/203, see 1987/137
investigation of, Mergers, Takeovers & Monopolies (Control) Act,1978
safeguards for shareholders and creditors, 63/204, see 1987/137

ANNUAL ACCOUNTS

information contained in, 63/VI, 63/395, 86
"true and fair" view of profit and loss, 63/VI/pl, 86/3

ANNUAL GENERAL MEETING

accounts, and, 63/148-AM 82/I, see 83/49 & 86/3, 63/159(1)-AM 82/I, 90B/43
auditor, 63/160-AM 90B/183, see 90B/185
auditors' report to be read at, 90B/193 (63/163(2) repealed by 90B/6)
business at, 63/148, 90B/193 (63/163(2) repealed by 90B/6)
duty to hold, 63/131
failure to hold, 63/131
frequency, 63/131
minutes of, 63/145(1)

continued

Annual general meeting continued
notice of, length of, 63/133, see 83/38(6) & 1987/137
provisions as to, 63/131-AM 82/I
registers of directors' and secretary's holdings of shares etc., to be produced at, 90B/60(9) (replacing 63/190(7))
resolution that meeting be treated as, 63/131(4)
to be held in the State, unless otherwise permitted, 63/140

ANNUAL REPORT OF THE MINISTER

to be laid before both Houses of the Oireachtas, 63/392

ANNUAL RETURN

company having a share capital, required to make, 63/125, 63/V
-provisions as to form, may be altered by Minister, 63/395(2)-AM 83/I
-not having a share capital, requirements in case of, 63/126
contents, 63/V
date of, 63/VpII
default in making, 63/127-AM 82/I-AM 90B/224
-striking off register, and, 82/12-AM 90B/245
directors, details of, in, 63/V
documents to be annexed to, 63/128-AM 82/I-AM 90B/244, see 86/7
failure to make, for two consecutive years, 82/12-AM 90B/245
filing requirements, 63/125
fine for default, 63/127-AM 82/I-AM 90B/244
matters to be included in, 63/125, 63/V
meaning of, 63/2(1)
members, when full list not required, 63/125(1)
private company, and, 63/125(1)
-certificates to be sent with, 63/129
public limited company need not give particulars of transfer, 63/125, 63/VpII note 2

continued

Annual return continued
signature of, 63/127 & 129
required to be filed within sixty days of annual general meeting, 63/127

APPEAL

refusal to register name of company, and, 63/21
stock exchange rejection of application for official listing, and, 1984/282, see 1991/18

APPLICATION

court, to, [see **Court**]
form of, for shares or debentures not to be issued except with prospectus, 63/44(3)
foreign company, for shares or debentures in, 63/365-AM 82/I
-penalty for contravening provisions as to, 63/365-AM 82/I
prospectus issued generally, in pursuance of, when revocable or voidable, 63/56(5)

APPLICATION FOR SHARES

revocability of, 63/56(5)

ARRANGEMENT OR COMPROMISE WITH CREDITORS OR MEMBERS

[see **Compromise or Arrangement**]
creditors, with, in voluntary winding up, 63/279
power to acquire shares of dissenters, 63/204, see 1987/137
sanction of court, with, 63/201-203, see 1987/137
-information to members or creditors, 63/202, see 1987/137 & 90/23(7)
-limits to, 63/201, see 1987/137
-meeting of members before, 63/201, see 1987/137

continued

Arrangement or compromise with creditors or members continued
-scheme for amalgamation of two or more companies, and, 63/203, see 1987/137
-scheme for reconstruction of company, and, 63/203, see 1987/137
voluntary winding up, on, when binding on company and creditors, 63/279
what included in expression, 63/201(7), see 1987/137
winding up by court, on, power of liquidator to make, 63/231

ARTICLES OF ASSOCIATION

Act, application of provisions in, overriding, 63/2(4)
adopt all or part of Table A, may, 63/13(1)
alteration of, provisions as to, 63/15
-court by in relief of minority, effect of, 63/205(4), see 90/5(4)
-members' liability, not to increase, 63/27
-relief, 63/78
-special resolution, by, 63/15
binding effect of, 63/25(1)
borrowing powers, and, 63/115, 83/6, see 1989/78
companies other than companies limited by shares, statutory forms of, 63/16-AM 82/17
company limited by shares, application of Table A to, 63/13(2)
constructive notice of, 63/8(1), 1973/163/6 [see also **Ultra Vires rule**]
contract between member and company, as, 63/25(1)
director, when person may not be appointed, 63/179-AM 82/I
enforcement of, 63/25(1)
enforcement of rights conferred by, 63/25(1)
form of, 63/14
legal requirement for, 63/11-AM 82/2, 63/13-AM 82/14
meaning of, 63/2(1)-AM 83/I
members entitled to copy of, 63/29-AM 83/I

continued

Articles of association continued
-and company, extent to which bound by, 63/25
-number of, to be stated in articles of company limited by guarantee and unlimited company, 63/12-AM 82/I
model forms, 63/A, B, C, D, E
printing of, 63/14
private company, of, 63/I (Table A pII)
procedure for variation of shareholders' rights, and, 63/78-AM 82/I, see 83/38(8) & 1987/137
public limited company, of, 63/I (Table A pI)
public document, 63/370
reconstruction by voluntary liquidation, and, 63/260, see 1987/137
registration of, 63/17, see 82/3 & 83/5
regulations of the company prescribing, when to be registered, 63/11-AM 82/2
resolutions, copies of what, to be annexed to, 63/143(2), see 83/18(6) & 39 & 53(1) & 55(1j)
signature of, by each subscriber, 63/14
Table A, adoption and application of, 63/13
unlimited company, 63/16, 63/I (Table E)

ASSETS

accounting principles and, 86/5 & 6
alternative accounting rules and, 86/S17-22
current, [see **Current Assets**]
distribution of, restrictions for public limited company, [see **Distributions**]
fixed, [see **Fixed Assets**]
fixed and current, how classified in accounts, 63/VIpI
floating charge, subject to, payment of certain debts in priority, 63/285(7)
fungible, meaning of and accounting treatment, 86/S15
historical cost accounting rules and, 86/S4-16
non-cash, [see **Non-cash Assets**]
unclaimed or undistributed, 63/307
winding up by court, collection and distribution of, 63/235 & 236
winding up by court, payment of costs out of, 63/244

ASSURANCE COMPANY

accounts of, and of wholly owned subsidiary of, 63/VIpIII
annual return of, 63/128(4), see 86/7(3)
realised profits of, 83/48, see 1989/78 & 90B/260(3)

ATTACHMENT

against company, in winding up by the court void, 63/219
creditor not entitled to benefit where company subsequently wound up, when, 63/291

AUDITORS

accountants, recognition of bodies of, 90B/191
- supplementary provisions, 90B/192
annual general meeting,
-where none appointed at, 63/160(4) & (5)-AM 82/I-AM 90B/183
-right to receive notice of and attend, 90B/193 (63/163 repealed by 90B/6)
appointment of, 63/160, 90B/183-184
-new, 63/161-AM 90B/184
approval of qualifications obtained outside the State, 90B/189
auditors, register of, 90B/198
- transitional provisions, 90B/199
- duty to keep registrar informed, 90B/200
- power of Minister to make supplementary regulations, 90B/201
authorisation of body of accountants by Minister, 90B/192
books, right of access to, 90B/193
director not to be, 90B/187 (63/162-AM 82/6 repealed by 90B/6)
directors' report, duty, 86/15
duties of, 90B/193 (63/163 repealed by 90B/6), (63/VII repealed by 90B/6)

continued

Auditors continued
disqualification from being, 90B/187 (63/162-AM 82/6 repealed by 90B/6)
false statement to, by officer, 90B/197
first, 63/160(6)
general meeting,
-requisition of, by resigning auditor, 90B/186
-right of attendance and audience, 90B/193 (63/163 repealed by 90B/6)
information, right to, 90B/193 (63/163 repealed by 90B/6)
investigation, duties of, in, 90B/10 (63/168 repealed by 90B/6)
liability of, avoidance of, certain provisions indemnifying against, 63/200
-relief from, by court in certain cases, 63/391
Minister, consultation regarding standards and qualifications, by, 90B/190
names and addresses of, to be stated in prospectus, 63/IIIpl/15
persons undergoing training on 1 January 1990, 90B/188
power in relation to subsidiaries, 90B/196
prohibition on acting while disqualification order in force, 90B/195
prosecution of officers and members, duties in, 63/299(4)
qualifications for appointment as, 90B/187 (63/162-AM 82/6 repealed by 90B/6)
removal of, 63/161-AM 90B/184, 90B/183-184
remuneration of, 63/160(8)
report to members, 90B/193
resignation of, 90B/185-186
resolutions relating to appointment and removal, 63/161-AM 90B/184
retiring, resolution against re-election of, extended notice of, 63/161-AM 90B/184
-representations by, 63/161(3) & (4), 90B/185-186
rights of, 90B/193 (63/163 repealed by 90B/6)

continued

Auditors continued
statement on re-registration of private company as public limited company, 83/9(3)
status of, 63/160
statutory duty of, 90B/193 (63/163 repealed by 90B/6)

AUDITORS' REPORT

accounts, not generally included in expression "document annexed to", 63/164
annual return, to be annexed to, 63/128, see 86/7(3)
balance sheet, to be attached to, 63/157
contents of, 90B/193 (63/163-AM 83/I repealed by 90B/6), (63/VII repealed by 90B/6)
copies of, who entitled to, 63/159
directors, when to include statement as to payments to, 63/191(8)
distributions, "relevant accounts", 83/49, see 1989/78
general meeting, to be read at, 90B/193 (63/163 repealed by 90B/6)
officers, when to include statement as to loans to, 90B/41-45 (63/192(3) cesser 90B/49)
prospectus, in, 63/III/19
publication of, with full accounts, 86/19

AUTHENTICATION OF DOCUMENTS

by officer of company, 63/42
when issued by Minister, 63/394

"AUTHORISED MINIMUM"

[see **Public limited company**]
meaning, 83/19, 83/2(1), see 1989/78
Minister may change amount, 83/19(2), see 1989/78

BALANCE SHEET

[see **Accounts**]
accounts and auditors' report to be annexed, 63/157-AM 82/I
banking company, of, [see **Bankers**]
"balance sheet date", 86/S61
comparative figures to be shown, 86/4(8)
copy of, to be annexed to annual return, 63/128, 86/7
-who entitled to, 63/159
current assets, 63/VI
date of, 83/2(1), 86/S61
directors' duty to prepare, 63/148
directors' report to be attached to, 63/158, see 86/13 & 19(4) & 25(5)
dividends in arrear, details of, 86/S25 & 35
documents to be annexed or attached to, 63/157-AM 82/I
exemptions from, 63/VI
false statements in, penalty for, 90B/242 (63/380 repealed by 90B/6)
fixed assets, 63/VI
form and contents of, 63/149, 63/VI, see 83/9(12 & 13a) & 49 & 86/3
format for, 86/S4
general meeting to be laid before company in, in every calendar year, 63/148(2)
group, [see **Group accounts**]
guarantees, details of, 86/S25 & 36
holding or subsidiary company, special provisions where company is, 63/VIpII
indebtedness, details of, 86/S25 & 34 & 35
investments, information to be given, 86/S25 & 31
members, right to receive copies, 63/159
"modified", for small or medium-sized company, 86/8(1-3)
notes to, 86/S25-37
provisions, 63/VI
publication of, 86/19
reference to, includes certain notes on, and documents annexed to, 63/149(8)

continued

Balance Sheet continued
reserves, 63/VI
revaluation reserve and, 86/S22
share capital and debentures, details of, 86/S25-28
signature of, 63/156, 86/18, see 83/9(13a) & 49
subsidiary, of, [see **Group accounts**]
taxation, details of provision for, 86/S25 & 33
unqualified report, meaning of, 83/9(13)

BANK HOLIDAY

meaning of, 63/2(1)

BANKERS

accounts of, provisions as to, 63/VIpIII, see 83/9(13b) & 90B/193
balance sheet of, signing of by three directors and secretary, 63/156(2)
books and papers of, application for inspection and, production of, 63/384(2)
business of, not to be carried on by partnership of more than ten persons, 63/372
company carrying on business of, privileges of, where places of business stated in annual return, 63/375
duties of, in investigation, 90B/10 (63/168(6) repealed by 90B/6)
-extent of, 90B/23(2) (63/173 repealed by 90B/6)
-in prosecutions of officers and members, 63/299(4)
licence granted by Central Bank, and, Central Bank Act, 1971/15
loans etc. to directors and others, 90B/44
meaning of, Central Bank Act, 1971/2
unlimited, proposing to register as limited, to give notice to customers, 63/373

BANKRUPT

effect of contributory becoming, 63/211
undischarged, not to be a director or be concerned in management of company, 90B/169 (replacing 63/183-AM 82/I)

BANKRUPTCY LAW

what provisions of, applicable to winding up of
insolvent company, 63/284

BILL OF EXCHANGE

name of company, and, 63/114-AM 82/I
how made, accepted or endorsed on behalf of
company, 63/39

BILL OF SALE

charge equivalent to, requires registration, 63/99

BODY CORPORATE

auditor, may not be, 90B/187 (63/162-AM 82/6 repealed
by 90B/6)
liquidator, may not be, 63/300
meaning of, 63/2(3)
member, cannot be, of its holding company, 63/32
receiver, may not be, 63/314-AM 82/I

BONUS SHARES

allotment, effect of requirements as to payment for
shares, 83/26(5) & 28
capital redemption reserve fund may be used in
paying up, (63/64(6)-AM 83/I cesser 90B/220)
not a "distribution", 83/51, see 1989/78
pre-emption rights not applicable, 83/23(13), see
1989/78
share premium account may be used for paying up,
63/62(2)-AM 82/I-AM 90B/23

BOOKS

account of, [see **Account, books of**]
and papers, application for production and inspection
of, 63/384

continued

Books continued
-company, and liquidator of, evidence in winding up, when, 63/304
-destruction or falsification of, 90B/243 (63/294 repealed by 90B/6)
-disposal of, on dissolution, 63/305
-order for delivery to liquidator in winding up by court, 63/236
-order for inspection of, 63/243, see 90B/251
computers, storage of records on, 77/4
evidence of matters recorded, 63/304
form of, 63/378, 77/4
liability of officers where proper books not kept, 90B/203-204
meaning, 63/2(1), 90B/3
minute, [see **Minutes**]
production to inspectors, 63/384, 90B/10
search of premises and retention of, 90B/20
security of, prohibition of disclosure by authorities, 90B/21

BOOK DEBTS

charge on, requires registration, 63/99(2)
deposit of negotiable instrument for securing, not a charge on, 63/99(6)

BORROWING

[see **Charges; Debentures**]
authorisation for, 63/115-AM 83/I
restriction on exercise of, 63/115

BUSINESS

commencement of, [see **Commencement of Business**]
fraudulent purpose, carried on for, 90B/137 (replacing 63/297)
place of, of foreign company, meaning of, 63/360
suspension for a year, ground for winding up, 63/213

BUSINESS LETTERS

corporate name etc., where business carried out under different name, Registration of Business Names Act, 1963
details to be included on, 1973/163/9
directors' names to be stated on, 63/196
where company in winding up, to state fact, 63/303
-receiver appointed, to state fact, 63/317

BUSINESS NAMES

Registration of Business Names Act, I963

CALLS

company, by, provisions in articles, 63/66
court, application by liquidator to, Rules Or74 r93-95
difference in times and amounts of, 63/66
made but not paid, charge on, requires registration, 63/99
winding up, by the court in, court may make, 63/238
-only to be made on, special resolution providing for, 63/67
-voluntary in, 63/276(1)

CAPACITY OF COMPANY TO ACT

Ultra vires rule restricted by statute, 1973/163/6

CAPITAL

[see **Capital Redemption Reserve; Share Capital**]
maintenance of, [see **Maintenance of capital**]
meeting to consider serious loss of, 83/40, see 1989/78 & 90B/260(2)
-penalties of failure to convene, 83/57(2)
redemption or purchase of shares out of [see **Purchase by company of its own shares; Redemption of shares**]

CAPITAL DUTY

Finance Act,1973/69-71, 63/395(2)-AM 83/I, 63/VIII, 1983/259

CAPITAL REDEMPTION RESERVE

general provisions as to, (63/64-AM 83/I cesser 90B/220)
utilisation of or reduction of, (63/64-AM 83/I cesser 90B/220)
[see **Financial Assistance by Company for Acquisition of its Shares**]

CAPITAL (SHARE)

allotment of, offered to public, 63/53
alterations to, 63/68
-consolidation of shares, 63/68
-conversion of shares into stock, 63/68
-increase in, procedure for, 63/68, 63/70-AM 82/I, see 1989/78 & 90B/260(1)
-notice of, to be given to registrar within one month, 63/69, see 1989/78 & 90B/221 & 260(1)
-reconversion of stocks into shares, 63/68
-sub-division of shares, 63/68
-unlimited company formed under Joint Stock Companies Acts by, 63/327(2)
amount of, to be stated in memorandum, 63/6(4), see 1989/78
application for, amount payable on, 63/53(3)-AM 83/I
"called up", 83/2(1)
consolidation, division of, and cancellation of unissued, 63/68
equity, meaning of, 63/155(5)
increase of, notice of, to be given to registrar within fifteen days, 63/70, see 1989/78
reduction of, [see **Reduction of Capital**]
stock, conversion into, 63/68
uncalled, charge on, requires registration, 63/99(2)
winding up, company may resolve that part of only to be called up on, 63/67

CERTIFICATES

private company, to be sent with annual return of, 63/129
shares, debentures and debenture stock, of company's obligation in respect of, 63/86
shares, of, prima facie evidence of title, 63/87-AM 77/5

CERTIFICATES OF EXEMPTION

meaning and effect of, 63/45
-in case of foreign company, 63/362

CERTIFICATE OF INCORPORATION

company not formed but registered under Act, or, 63/336-AM 83/I
conclusive evidence of certain matters, 83/11 & 14 (63/19 repealed 83/III)
effect of, 63/18(2)
inspection of, and copies of, 63/370
new, on change of name, 63/23(3)
official notification of issue, 1973/163/4
public limited company, statement that company is, 83/5, see 1989/78
registrar to give, 63/18
registration of memorandum, issue on, 63/18

CERTIFICATE OF REGISTRATION

to be given by registrar of charge, 63/104

CERTIFICATION OF TRANSFER

meaning and effect of, 63/85

CHAIRMAN

minute signed by, evidence of proceedings, 63/145(2)
of meeting, election of, where no provision in articles, 63/134(d)

CHAMBER OF COMMERCE

effect of revocation of licence by Minister where name contains words, 63/24(8)

CHARGES

acquisition of property subject to a charge, 63/101-AM 82/I
book debts, on, registration of, 63/99
calls made but not paid, registration of, 63/99
certificate by registrar as to registration of, 63/104
copies of instruments creating, to be kept by company, 63/109
copyright, on, registration of, 63/99
created or evidenced by instrument which if executed by an individual would be registerable as a bill of sale, registration of, 63/99
enforcement of security, duty to notify registrar, 63/107-AM 82/I
existing charge on acquired property, 63/101-AM 82/I
extension of time for registering or correction of error in registered particulars of, 63/106
failure to register, security void against liquidator etc., 63/99(1)
floating, [see **Floating Charge**]
foreign companies, by, registration of, 63/99
foreign property, on, 63/99(3)
goodwill, on, registration of, 63/99
inspection by members etc. of company's register and copies of instruments, 63/110
land, on, registration of, 63/99
meaning of, 63/99(10)
mortgage, "charge" includes, 63/99(10)
patent, on, registration of, 63/99
public limited company, on own shares, 83/44
register of, kept by company to be open to inspection, 63/110
registration of, [see **Registration of Charges**]
release or satisfaction, 63/105

continued

Changes continued
required to be registered with registrar, 63/99 & 101
-by whom to be registered, 63/100
-copy of, to be kept at company's registered office, 63/109
-copy of, to be open to inspection, 63/110
securing issue of debentures, for, registration of, 63/99
ships, on, registration of, 63/99-AM 90B/122
statutory declaration verifying release or satisfaction, 63/105
trademark, on, registration of, 63/99
unregistered, effect, 63/99

CHEQUE

name of company, and, 63/114-AM 82/I

CHILD

meaning, 90B/3

CLASS

identification of, in register of members, 63/116
meeting, corporation, how represented at, 63/139
-resolutions of, registration of, and copies of, 63/143
-proxies at, 63/136(7)
members of, rights of, when not to be varied by alteration of memorandum, 63/28(3)
rights of, to be registered if not in memorandum etc., 83/39
shares of, variation of rights of, 63/78, 83/38, see 1987/137

CLASSIFICATION OF COMPANIES

general provisions, 63/5
indication of, in company name, 63/6-AM 83/I, see 1989/78 & 90B/253
"old public company", 83/2(1) & 12(1)

COLLECTIVE CITATION

shall be construed as one Act and may be cited together as, "Companies Acts, 1963 to 1990", 90B/1(2)

COMMENCEMENT OF ACTS

Companies Act, 1963, 63/1(2), 1 April 1964
Companies (Amendment) Act, 1977, 77/11(3), 1 April 1978
Companies (Amendment) Act, 1982, 82/24(3), 3 August 1982
Companies (Amendment) Act, 1983, 83/1(3), 13 October 1983
Companies (Amendment) Act, 1986, 86/25(4),1 August 1986 (except ss 7(1)(a)(ii) and 8(7) & (8))
Companies (Amendment) Act, 1990, 29 August 1990
Companies Act, 1990, 90B/2, 27 December 1990 (only in respect of ss 1-5, 107-121, 180 (other than subsections 1g, 2 & 3), 181, 235, 238-240, 242, 244, 245, 247), 90B/2, 1 February 1991 (only in respect of ss 15, 16, 19-21, 23-27, 29-49, 52, 243, 252-262)

COMMENCEMENT OF BUSINESS

not taking place for a year, ground for winding up, 63/213
public limited company, certificate issued by registrar, 83/6, see 1989/78 & 90B/256
-offence relating to, 83/6, see 1989/78
-statutory declaration to be lodged, 83/6, see 1989/78
public limited company, 63/115-AM 83/l
restrictions on, 63/115-AM 82/l-AM 83/l

COMMENCEMENT OF WINDING UP

in winding up, by the court, 63/220
-voluntary, 63/253

COMMISSION

assets, not to be treated as, 86/4(12)
restrictions on payment in respect of subscriptions for shares, 63/59-AM 82/I
to subscribers for shares or persons procuring subscriptions, when lawful, 63/59-AM 82/I

COMMITTEE OF INSPECTION

winding up, court, by
-appointment of, how applied for and made, 63/232
-constitution, proceedings, etc. of, 63/233
-sanction of, required for exercise of certain powers of liquidators, 63/231(1)
winding up, voluntary
-appointment of and provisions as to, 63/268

COMMON CONTROL

meaning of, Mergers, Takeovers & Monopolies (Control) Act, 1978/1

COMPANIES (CONSOLIDATION) ACT, 1908

construction of references to company registered under, in other Acts, 63/4
repealed, 63/XII

COMPANIES ACT, 1959

repeal of provisions of, 63/3 & XII

COMPANIES ACTS

proceedings taken, etc., under former, not affected, 63/3(2)

COMPANIES INCORPORATED OUTSIDE IRELAND

[see **Foreign companies**]

COMPANIES LIQUIDATION ACCOUNT

in Bank of Ireland, 63/307

COMPANIES NOT FORMED UNDER ACT

application of Act to, formed and registered under former Acts, 63/324
-registered but not formed under former Acts, 63/325
-unlimited companies re-registered as "limited" under former Acts, 63/326
memorandum and articles, may substitute for deed of settlement, 63/341
provisions as to, 90B/S (replacing 63/IX)
registration of, 63/328
-certificate of, 63/336-AM 83/I
-documents to be delivered to registrar on, verification of, 63/332
-effect of, 63/340-AM 83/I
-evidence, registrar may require what, on, 63/333
-joint stock, requirements for, 63/330-AM 83/I
.other than, requirements for, 63/331
.what is, for purposes of, 63/329
-liabilities previously existing not affected by, 63/338
-name of, provisions as to, on, 63/334
-"limited" to be part of, on, 63/335-AM 83/I
-proceedings, continuance of, notwithstanding, 63/339
-vesting of property on, 63/337
-stay of proceedings against, provisions as to on presentation of winding up petition, after, 63/342
-on winding up order, after, 63/343

COMPANY

defunct, may be struck off register, 63/311-AM 82/12-AM 90B/245
-restoration to register of, 63/311(8), 90B/246
directors, must have two, 63/174
dissolved, disposal by registrar of documents relating to, 63/313

continued

Company continued
"existing", meaning of, 63/2(1)
-application of Act to, 63/324
flotation, [see **Flotation of Company**]
foreign, [see **Foreign Company**]
-may dispense with use of word "limited" when, 63/24
incorporation, date of, 63/18
-how formed, 63/5
investigation of affairs of, and of person interested in, [see **Investigations**]
joint stock, [see **Joint Stock Companies**]
law governing, [see **Abbreviations, terms used and references**]
limited, may re-register under Act, 83/52 (63/20 cesser 83/54)
meaning of, 63/2(1), 63/376
members, effect of having less than minimum number (public seven, private two), 63/36
offer of shares or debentures to public prohibited, of private company having a share capital, 83/21
pre-incorporation contracts, 63/37
private, 63/33(1)
private, [see **Private Company**]
public company limited by guarantee, and having a share capital, prohibition on further formations, 83/7
purchase of own shares or shares in holding company, may not give financial assistance for, 63/60, see 1989/78 & 90B/155 & 224 & 260(1)
registration under Act by companies other than joint stock companies, 63/331
returns, enforcement of duty to make, 63/371
secretary, must have, 63/175
service on, how effected, 63/379
shares freely transferable, [see **Shares**]
subscription of own shares or shares in holding company, may not give financial assistance for, 63/60, see 1989/78 & 90B/155 & 224 & 260(1)
unable to pay its debts, may be wound up, 63/213
-when deemed to be, 63/214-AM 90B/123

continued

Company continued
unlimited, [see **Unlimited Company**]
winding up, grounds for, 63/213
-may petition for own, 63/215

COMPANY LAW

Statutes, rules and regulations comprising
[see **Abbreviations, terms used and references**]

COMPANY LIMITED BY GUARANTEE

articles of, must be registered, 63/11-AM 82/2
-statutory forms of, 63/16, Table D, see 82/14
-to state number of members, 63/12(2)
management by committee or council, 63/174 & 176
meaning of, 63/5(2)
members of, notice of increase of, 63/12(3)
memorandum of, statutory form of, 63/16, Tables C, D
memorandum, requirements as to, 63/16
share capital, having, liability of members of, on winding up, 63/207(3)
-share capital, having, meaning, 63/26
-share capital, public limited company having, no longer capable of formation, 83/7
-not having, profits of, may only be divided among members as such, 63/26
-when deemed to have, 63/26(2)

COMPANY LIMITED BY SHARES

articles of, may be registered, 63/11-AM 82/2
meaning of, 63/5(2)
memorandum of, statutory form of, 63/16, Table B
Table A, when applicable to, 63/13

COMPENSATION FOR LOSS OF OFFICE OF DIRECTOR

in connection with transfer of undertaking, 63/187
-of shares, 63/188

continued

Compensation for loss of office of director continued
particulars as to, to be given in accounts, 63/191, see 86/S49
payment by company of, 63/186
what deemed to be, 63/189

COMPROMISE OR ARRANGEMENT

between company and creditors or members, 63/201, see 83/30(14a) & 83/38(10) & 1987/137
notice of meetings in connection with, 63/202-AM 82/I, see 1987/137 & 90/23(7)
-reconstruction or amalgamation, involving, 63/203, see 83/38(10) & 1987/137

COMPUTER

use of, for certain company records, 77/4

CONNECTED PERSON

meaning, 90B/3

CONSISTENCY - ACCOUNTING PRINCIPLE

requirement, 86/5

CONSOLIDATED ACCOUNTS

[see **Group Accounts**]

CONSOLIDATION

share capital of, [see **Capital**]

CONTRACTS

company on behalf of, how made, 63/38
constituting title of allottee, 63/58
debentures for, specific performance of, 63/97
continued

Contracts continued
directors interested in, how to give notice, 63/194-AM 82/I, see 90B/27(3) & 47
disclaimer of unprofitable, in winding up, 63/290
evidenced in writing, 63/38
form of, 63/38
prospectus, referred to in, provisions as to, 63/47(1) & 63/IIIpl
-statutory meeting required to approve variation of, (63/48 repealed 83/III)
pre-incorporation
-effect of, 63/37
-ratification of, 63/37
provisional only, before company entitled to commence business, 63/115(4)
receiver appointed out of Court, liability of, on, 63/316(2)
rescinding of, in winding up, 63/290(6)
seal, under, 63/38
writing, in, 63/38

CONTRIBUTORIES

adjustment of rights of, and distribution of surplus to, 63/242
arrest of absconding, 63/247
application to court in voluntary winding up, by, 63/280, see 90B/131
bankrupt becoming, 63/211
calls made to extent of liability, 63/235(3), Rules Or74 r93 to 95
calls may be made on, by Court, 63/238
death of, 63/210
destruction or falsification of books by, 90B/243 (63/294-AM 82/I repealed by 90B/6)
enforcement of liability of, 63/235
inspection of company books by, order for, 63/243, see 90B/251
liability of past and present members as, 63/207
-a speciality debt, 63/209
liquidator's books, may inspect, 63/243, see 90B/251

continued

Contributories continued
list of, to be settled, in winding up by the Court, 63/235
in voluntary winding up, 63/276(1)
meaning of, 63/208
meeting of, [see **Meetings**]
order against, for payment, when may be made, 63/237
-evidence of what matters, 63/240
order by court on, conclusive evidence, 63/240
payment of amount due, order for, 63/237 & 239
person wrongfully stating himself to be, 63/224(7)
set-off by, 63/237
unregistered company, in winding up of, 63/346
winding up, when may petition for, 63/215
-in, court to have regard to wishes of, 63/309

COPYRIGHT

charge on, or licence under, requires registration, 63/99

CORPORATION

meaning of, 63/2(3)
represented at meetings, how, 63/139

COSTS

court may order security for, to be given in action by limited company, 63/390
winding up, by the court of, 63/244
-voluntary of, 63/281

COUNSEL

not included in the expression "agent", 63/2(1)

COURT

alternative relief to winding up, petition to, for, 63/205-AM 82/I, see 90/5(4)

continued

Court continued
application to
-alteration of objects, to cancel, 63/10
-alteration of other matters in memorandum, to cancel, 63/28
-auditors, as to representations of retiring, 63/161(4)
-bankrupt, for leave for, to act as director, 90B/169 (replacing 63/183)
-certificates or debentures, to compel company to issue, 63/86(3)
-class rights, to cancel variation of, 63/78
-director proposed to be removed, as to representations of, 63/182(4)
-dissolution of company, void, for declaration that, 63/310
-investigations, for examination on oath in, 90B/10 (replacing 63/168(4))
-private company, relief from consequences of failure to comply with provisions necessary to constitute, for, 63/34(2)
-rectification
.of register of charges, for, 63/106(1)
.of register of members, for, 63/122
-reduction of capital, for, 63/73
-relief against liability for costs, 63/391
-restoration of company to the register, for, 63/311(8), 90B/246
-returns, to enforce duty to make, 63/371
-shares at discount, for sanction to issue of, (63/63 repealed 83/III) but see 83/27(4)
-shareholder dissenting from scheme for transfer of shares by, 63/204, see 1987/137
-time, extension of, for delivery of documents in connection with allotment, 63/58(4)
.for registration of charge, 63/106
-voluntary winding up in, 63/280
.compromise or arrangement, powers of in connection with, 63/201, see 1987/137
.involving reconstruction or amalgamation, powers of in connection with, 63/203, see 1987/137

continued

Court continued
disclaimer of unprofitable contracts, etc., by liquidator, leave of, necessary for, 63/290
fraudulent preference, jurisdiction of, in application with respect to, 63/287(3)
Judge of, application to, for inspection and production of books, 63/384
meaning of, 90B/235 (63/2(1)-AM 90B/235)
-in connection with provisions as to receiver, 63/319(3)
order of
-compelling inspection
.of copies of charges, 63/110(3)
.of minutes of general meeting, 63/146(4)
.of register of debenture holders and trust deed, 63/92(5)
.of register of directors and secretary, 90B/51(13) (replacing 63/195(11))
.of register of members, 63/119(4)
-director, prohibiting person from being, 90B/160 (63/184 repealed by 90B/6)
-investigation, for, 90B/7 (replacing 63/166)
-meeting, to call, 63/135
powers conferred on, by Act as to proceeding against contributories or debtors cumulative, 63/248
receiver, appointed out of court, may apply to, for directions, 90B/171 (replacing 63/316(1))
-default of, as to returns, application to, on, 63/322
-information to be given to by, and powers of, as to, 63/319 & 320
-remuneration of, may fix, 63/318
statement of company's affairs to be filed in, 63/224, see 90B/18
winding up by, and application to in, [see **Winding Up, Court, by**]

COURT PROTECTION

[see **Examiner**]

"c.p.t."

public limited company with name in Irish may use abbreviation, 83/4

CREDITORS

application of rules in bankruptcy, 63/284
application to Court by, in voluntary winding up, 63/280, see 90B/131
arrangement with, in voluntary winding up, 63/279 [see **Compromise or Arrangement**]
arrangement or compromise with, on a winding up, liquidator's powers, 63/231
arrangement with, on a winding up, when binding, 63/279
assignment by company for benefit of, void, 90B/135(2) (replacing 63/286(3))
concealment of name, on reduction of share capital, 63/77
debts which can be proved, 63/215, 63/283
delivery of documents to registrar, may apply to court to enforce company's duty as to, 63/371
inspection of books by, order for, 63/243
meetings of, [see **Meetings**]
meeting of, on a creditors' winding up, 63/266-AM 82/I-AM 90B/130, 63/272-AM 82/I
meeting of, on a members' winding up, 90B/129 (replacing 63/261-AM 82/I)
person untruthfully stating himself to be, 63/224(7)
preferential debts, list of, 63/285-AM 82/10-AM 90B/134
procedure for ascertaining, Rules Or74 r96-100 & 102
procedure for proving claims, Rules Or74 r96-100 & 102
proof by, time for, may be fixed, 63/241
ranking of claims, on a winding up, 63/284
reduction of capital, provisions as to, 63/73(2) & 74
-rights of, on, where ignorant of, 63/76(2)
restriction of enforcement rights, on a winding up, 63/291

continued

Creditors continued
time limit for proof of debts on a winding up, power of court to set, 63/241
winding up, petition may be presented by, or by prospective or contingent creditor, 63/215
wishes of, court to have regard to in winding up, 63/309

"CREDIT TRANSACTION"

disclosure of, 90B/41-47
-auditor's duty in breach of, 90B/46
-exclusions, 90B/45
meaning, 90B/25(1 & 3)

"CUIDEACHTA PHOIBLI THEORANTA"

name of public limited company in Irish must end with, 83/4

CURRENT ASSETS

general provisions for determining costs or expenses of, 86/S10-16 & 60
historical cost accounting rules and, 86/S10 & 11
meaning of, in accounts, 86/S60

CURRENT COST ACCOUNTING

[see **Alternative accounting rules**]

DAMAGES

compensation for loss of office, not included in, 63/189(3)
director removed by ordinary resolution may be entitled to, 63/182(7)

DEBENTURE HOLDERS

action by individual where series issued, Rules Or15 r9
alteration of company's objects, notice of, to be given to certain, 63/10(7)
balance sheet, entitled to copy of, 63/159
compromise or arrangement affecting rights of, 63/202(2), see 1987/137 & see 90/23(7)
existing, issue of prospectus to, 63/44(7)
register of, 63/91
-inspection and copies of, 63/92
-place where, to be kept, provisions as to, 63/91
-power to keep on computer, 77/4
trust deed, right of, to require copy of, 63/92
trustee for, restrictions on exemption from liability of, 63/93

DEBENTURES

allotment of, prohibited in certain cases unless statement in lieu of prospectus delivered, 63/54
application for and allotment of, in pursuance of prospectus issued generally, 63/56
balance sheet, in, 86/S note 5 balance sheet formats
bonus issue, not from capitalisation of unrealised profits, 83/45(3), see 1989/78
certificates of, company's obligations as to, 63/86
charge for securing, requires registration, 63/99
commission allowance or discount paid to subscriber or person procuring subscriptions for, particulars of, to be given to registrar, 63/99(9)
conditions to be met before admitted to official stock exchange listing, 1984/282, see 1991/18
contract to take, may be specifically enforced, 63/97
directors interested in, register of, 63/190
floating charge, secured by, [see **Floating Charge**]
floating charge, secured by, preferential debts, 63/94
form of application for, to be issued with prospectus, 63/44(3)
irredeemable, may be, 63/94

continued

Debentures continued
listing particulars, and, 1984/282, see 1991/18
meaning of, 63/2(1)
mortgage and, 63/94
offer to public, allotment with a view to, 63/51, see 83/21(2)
offer to public, requirement for prospectus, 63/44-47 & III, see 90B/221 [see **Offer of Shares or Debentures to Public; Prospectus**]
perpetual, validity of, 63/94
private company, prohibition on offer to public, 83/21
public, meaning of offer to, 63/61
quotation for, 1984/282, see 1991/18
redeemed, re-issue of, 63/95-96
reissued, rights of mortgagee, 63/95
secured by charge, duty to register, 63/99, [see **Charges**]
secured by floating charge, preferential debts, 63/94
trustees, and, 63/93
stock exchange, allotment of debentures intended to be listed on, 63/57-AM 82/I
transfer of, refusal, 63/84-AM 82/I
uniform with those already dealt in on Stock Exchange, prospectus in connection with, 63/44(7)

DEBTS

concealment or misrepresentation, on a reduction of capital, 63/77-AM 82/I
inability to pay, ground for winding up, 63/213
-what deemed to be, 63/214-AM 90B/123
liability for, membership below minimum, 63/36
member, money payable by, under memorandum, 63/25
priority, having, in winding up or when receiver appointed, [see **Preferential Payments**]
proof of, [see **Proof**]

DECLARATION OF SOLVENCY

directors making, without reasonable grounds, 90B/128 (replacing 63/256(6)-AM 82/I)
necessary to constitute members' winding up, 90B/128 (replacing 63/256)

DEED

of company, execution of, outside the State, 63/40

DEED OF SETTLEMENT

substitution of memorandum and articles for, 63/341

DEFAMATORY MATTER

in representations
-of director proposed to be removed, 63/182(4)
-of retiring auditor, 63/161(4)

DEFERRED SHARES

prospectus to give details, 63/III/1

DEFUNCT COMPANY

[see **Dissolved company**]
registrar may strike off register, 63/311-AM 82/11-AM 82/12-AM 90B/245

DEPRECIATION

alternative accounting rules and, 86/S20
historical cost accounting rules, 86/S4-9
revaluation reserve, 86/S22

DEVELOPMENT COSTS

capitalisation of, accounting rules, 86/S8
treatment of, in calculating profits available for distribution, 86/20

DIRECTORS

[see **Officer**]
accounting records etc., duty, 90B/202
accounts, duty to prepare and lay etc., 63/148, see 86/3, 86/7 & 18 & 90B/43
acts of, valid, notwithstanding defect in appointment or qualification, 63/178
addresses of, 90B/51 (replacing 63/195)
age, duty to disclose, 90B/51
agent of company, as, relief from liability, and, 63/200-AM 83/I & 63/391
allotment of shares by, authority required for, 83/20
allotment of shares, personal liability for contravention of minimum subscription etc. requirements, 63/55-AM 82/I, see 83/22(2)
appointment of, 63/180-181
-approval of company in general meeting, 63/181
.to be voted on individually, 63/181
-by articles or advertisement of, restriction on, 63/179
-in place of removed director, 63/182(2)
assignment of office, requires special resolution, 63/199
auditor, may not be, 90B/187(3) (63/162-AM 82/6 repealed by 90B/6)
bankrupt, undischarged, may not be, 90B/169 (replacing 63/183-AM 82/I)
body corporate may not be, 63/176
casual vacancy in, arises on removal by ordinary resolution, when, 63/182(5)
change among, to be notified to registrar, 90B/51 (replacing 63/195(6)-AM 82/8)
company must have two, 63/174
compensation for loss of office
-aggregate amount to be shown in accounts, 63/191(1)
-general provisions as to, 63/189
-payment by company, 63/186
-transfer of shares, on, 63/188
-transfer of undertaking, on, 63/187

continued

Directors continued
compromise or arrangement, duties of, as to, 63/202(6), see 1987/137 & 90/23(7)
-interests of, to be disclosed in notices of meeting held in connection with, 63/202, see 1987/137 & 90/23(7)
contract of employment of, 63/182
contracts, duty of disclosure of interest, 90B/47
contracts with company, disclosure of, 63/194-AM 82/I, see 90B/27(3) & 47
court may prohibit certain persons from being, 90B/160 (63/184 repealed by 90B/6)
disclosure, duty of, as to certain matters, 63/193-AM 90B/53(11)
dividends, [see **Distributions; Dividends**]
emoluments of, aggregate to be shown in accounts, 63/191(1)
emoluments of, tax free prohibited, 63/185
employees, duty owed to company to have regard to interests of, 90B/52
falsification of books by, 90B/243
first statement by, on registration, 82/3
foreign company of, meaning of, 63/360
fraudulent trading
-civil liability, 90B/138 (90/33 deleted 90B/180)
-criminal liability, 90B/137 (90/34 deleted 90B/180)
indemnity out of assets, in defending certain proceedings, 63/200-AM 83/I
insolvent companies, disqualification order, [see **Disqualification Order**]
insurance company of, proposal to appoint must be notified to the Minister for approval, s 20 Insurance Act 1989
interested, disclosure by, 63/194, see 90B/27(3) & 47
issue of shares, statutory restrictions on powers to, 83/20
-liability in relation to allotment of shares, 63/56
-special remedy when company wound up, 90B/142 (replacing 63/298)
liability of, allotment, for compensation in respect of irregular, 63/55-AM 83/I

continued

Directors continued
-applicants, to repay money to, when, 63/53(4), see 83/22(2 & 3b)
-meetings, failure to convene on requisition, for, 63/132(5)
-permission to deal not granted, where, 63/57(2)
-prospectus, issue of, without necessary consents, for, 63/49(6)
-for mis-statements in, 63/49
-unlimited, extent of in winding up, 63/207(2), 63/237(2)
.may be if memorandum so provides, 63/197
.resolution for making, 63/198
liability of, avoidance provisions void, 63/200-AM 83/I
liability, when unlimited, 63/197-AM 82/I
life (governing, permanent), 63/182
loans to, to be shown in accounts, 90B/41-43 (63/192 cesser 90B/49)
meaning of, 63/2(1)
meetings, of, minutes of, to be kept, 63/145-AM 82/I, see 90B/27(3)
minimum of two required, 63/174
names of, 90B/51 (replacing 63/195), 82/3
nationalities of, 90B/51 (replacing 63/195), 82/3
number of, 63/174
occupations of, 90B/51 (replacing 63/195), 82/3
offences by, on or before a winding up, 63/293, 90B/243 (replacing 63/294)
particulars to appear in business letters, 63/196-AM 82/I
payments for loss of office, [see **Compensation for loss of office of director**]
payments to, to be disclosed, 63/189(4)
pensions of, accounts to show aggregate, 63/191(1b)
person in accordance with whose directions, accustomed to act, 63/2(2) & 125(3) & 196/6, 90B/51 (replacing 195(12)), 90B/57
prohibited from becoming, persons, 90B/160 (63/184 repealed by 90B/6), 63/176, 90B/169 (replacing 63/183), 90B/187 (replacing 63/162-AM 82/6)
prosecution of, on a winding up, 63/299-AM 90B/143

continued

Directors continued
prospectus, advertisement of name in, restrictions, 63/179-AM 82/I
prospectus, civil liability for mis-statement, 63/49
publication of information relating to, 90B/51 (replacing 63/195)
public limited company options, dealing in, [see **Directors' interests in shares etc.**]
qualification shares, not obtaining, 63/180, see 90B/110
reckless trading, civil liability, 90B/138
register of, and of secretary
-inspection of, 63/195
-particulars to be entered in, 90B/51 (replacing 63/195)
-shares and debentures in which, interested, 90B/53-57 & 59 (replacing 63/190)
relief from liability as, 63/200-AM 83/I
removal of, by ordinary resolution, 63/182
-representations on, 63/182(3)
remuneration of, may not be tax free, 63/185
report of, not a document annexed to the accounts, 63/164
-provisions as to, 63/158
responsibility for untrue statement in prospectus, 63/49
-onus of proof, 63/49
restrictions on becoming, 90B/169 (replacing 63/183), 63/176, 90B/187 (replacing 63/162(5a)-AM 82/6), 90B/160 (63/184 repealed by 90B/6)
retiring, when provisions do not apply for reappointment of, 63/181(4)
returns as to, 90B/51 (replacing 63/195-AM 82/8)
salaries of, particulars to be annexed to accounts, 63/191
salaries etc., [see **Emoluments**]
secretary who is a, may not act in dual capacity, when, 63/177
service contracts, copies to be available for inspection, 90B/50
service contracts, restrictions on, 90B/28
"shadow director", 90B/27

continued

Directors continued
substantial property transactions involving, restrictions, 90B/29
transactions involving, disclosure requirements [see **Loans etc. to directors and connected persons**]
unlimited liability of, 63/197-AM 82/I & 198
validity of acts, where appointment defective, 63/178
voluntary winding up
-creditors, cessation of powers of, on, 63/269(3)
-members, cessation of powers of, on, 63/258(2)

DIRECTORS' INTERESTS IN SHARES ETC.

directors' report, disclosure in, 90B/63
duty of director to notify company in writing of interests in shares or debentures, 90B/53 & 58
-circumstances in which duty is not discharged, 90B/57
-interests to be disregarded, 90B/55
-non-discharge of, 90B/53
-shadow directors, extension of provisions to, 90B/53(9)
-spouses and minor children, extension to interest and dealings of, 90B/64
-time limit, 90B/56
interests in shares or debentures, details required in notification, 90B/53
interest in shares or debentures, meaning, 90B/54
investigation of dealings in shares etc., 90B/66 [see **Investigations**]
options in listed shares or debentures of company, offence to deal in, 90B/30
-extension to agents, 90B/30(5)
recognised stock exchange, duty of company with dealing facilities to notify receipt of director's notification, 90B/65
register of directors' interest in shares and debentures
-entries, removal of, 90B/61
-entries, when not to be removed, 90B/62

continued

Directors' interests in shares etc. continued
-form of, 90B/60
shares and debentures in holding company etc., extension of provisions to, 90B/53(1)

DIRECTORS' REPORT

acquisition of own shares, particulars in, 86/14-AM 90B/233, see 1989/78
additional matters to be in, 86/13
auditors, duty to check, 86/15
balance sheet, to be attached to, 86/7
consistency with accounts, 86/15
members, right to receive copies, 63/159
power to include matters required to be covered in accounts, 86/24
safety statement, must contain evaluation of extent to which policy set out therein was fulfilled during the period covered by the report, s 12(6), Safety, Health and Welfare at Work Act, 1989

DISCLAIMER

leasehold property, of, 63/290(8)
onerous property and unprofitable contracts, of, 63/290
person injured by, proof by, 63/290(9)

DISCLOSURE OF INTEREST IN SHARES OF PUBLIC LIMITED COMPANY

[see **Directors' interests in shares etc.; Investigation by public limited company of interests in its shares**]
agent, acquisition through, 90B/79
"concert party" agreement
-interests held by each party attributed to other parties, 90B/73-74 & 76
-party acquiring (etc.) an interest in shares required to notify other parties, 90B/75

continued

Disclosure of interest in shares of public limited company continued
corporate interest, extension of provisions, 90B/72 & 76
duty to notify company of acquisition etc. of interest in its shares, 90B/67-79
interest in shares, meaning for notification provisions, 90B/72(2) & 74(2) & 76 & 77
interests in shares, percentage holding for notification requirement, 90B/70
interests to be disclosed, 90B/68-69
interests to be disregarded, 90B/78
notification to company, details to be given, 90B/71 & 74 & 79
-relief by court, 90B/79(4)
offences, 90B/79(7)
"percentage level", 90B/69
public limited company investigations, 90B/81
-on requisition of members, 90B/83
-penalties for failure to provide further information, 90B/85
-report to members, 90B/84
recognised stock exchange
-annual report of, 90B/93
-co-operation between Member States, 90B/96
-duty to notify certain interests, 90B/91 & 93
.duty of relevant authority to report contravention to Director of Public Prosecutions, 90B/92
-immunity from suit, 90B/95
-interpretation, 90B/90
-obligation of professional secrecy, 90B/94
register of interests in shares, duty of company to keep, 90B/80 & 82 & 86 & 87
register of interests in shares, inspection and provision of copies, 90B/80 & 88
"relevant share capital", 90B/67(2)
spouses and children, extension to interests held by, 90B/72 & 76
transitional provisions etc., 90B/106

DISCLOSURE ORDERS

applicable to, 90B/97
application, mode of, 90B/99
contravention, civil liability for, 90B/104
court
-made by, 90B/98
-powers of, 90B/101
effect of, 90B/98
information given, court's discretion to disclose, 90B/103
notice of, publication of, 90B/102(2)
notice of to be given to
-non-resident holder of shares or debentures in respect of which order is made, 90B/102(1)
-registrar, 90B/102(1)
-registered office of company, 90B/102(1)
-such other person as court sees fit, 90B/102(1)
scope of, 90B/100

DISCOUNT

company, special provisions as to accounts of, 63/VIpIII
issue of shares at, prohibition of, 83/27
shares may not be issued at, 63/59(2)
-except with sanction of court etc., (63/63 repealed 83/III) see 83/27(4)

DISQUALIFICATION ORDER

application for relief from, 90B/160(8)
court
-information to be given by directors to, 90B/166
-particulars to be supplied by to registrar, 90B/167
"default order", 90B/159
defence to charge of offence, 90B/150(2)
director of insolvent company
-may apply to court for relief, 90B/152(1 & 2)
.liquidator may appear and give evidence, 90B/152(4)

continued

Disqualification order continued
-may not act as director or secretary of new company unless capital conditions met, 90B/150
-notice of, by liquidator to registrar, 90B/151(1)
-register of, to be kept by registrar, 90B/153
.relief, entry of, 90B/153(2)
.removal from, 90B/153(3 & 4)
-restriction on, 90B/150
-shadow directors, application to, 90B/149(5)
disqualified persons, acting under directions of, penalty for, 90B/164
-civil liability for, 90B/165
-register of, to be kept by registrar, 90B/168
.relief, entry of, 90B/168(2)
.removal after five years, 90B/168(3)
enforcement, 90B/161-169
meaning, 90B/159
new company
-director of insolvent company subject to order must notify new company at its registered office before appointment, 90B/155(5)
-duty of liquidator to inform court of opinion that director of insolvent company may place new company in jeopardy, 90B/151(2)
-minimum allotted share capital, 90B/150(3)
.allotment, requirements as to, 90B/156
.amount to be paid, requirements as to, 90B/150(3)
.cash payment, requirement for, 90B/150(3)
.Minister may vary amounts, 90B/158
.prohibited transactions, relief for, 90B/157
-restrictions on, 90B/155
offences in connection with management etc. of a company, 90B/161
-civil liability for, 90B/163
period of, 90B/162
prohibition from acting as director, auditor, receiver, liquidator, examiner or managing company, 90B/160
receivership, application in, 90B/154

DISSENTING MEMBERS

objects, to alteration of, 63/10
to sale for consideration other than cash in winding up, 63/260(3), see 1987/137
to scheme approved by majority, acquisition of shares of, 63/204, see 1987/137
variation of rights, application by, to cancel, 63/78

DISSOLUTION OF COMPANY

after winding up, 63/249 & 263 & 273
books and papers, disposal of, on, 63/305
in creditors' voluntary winding up, 63/273(4 & 5)
in members' voluntary winding up, 63/263(4 & 5)
order for, in winding up by the court, 63/249
striking off register by, 63/311-AM 82/II, see 82/12-AM, 90B/245
void, court may declare, 63/310

DISSOLVED COMPANY

revival of, 63/311(8), 90B/246
assets of, become property of Minister for Finance on dissolution, s 28, State Property Act, 1954

DISTRESS

preferential payments first charge on property taken in, prior to winding up when, 63/285
void against company in winding up by the court, 63/219

DISTRIBUTABLE PROFITS

[see **Distributions**]
Payments required to be made out of, [see **Financial assistance by company for acquisition of its shares; Purchase by company of its own shares; Redemption of shares**]

DISTRIBUTIONS

[see **Dividends**]
conditions restricting, 83/45-51, see 1989/78
development expenditure, treatment of in calculating permitted distribution, 86/20

DISTRIBUTION OF ASSETS

restrictions on, 83/51, 83/45-AM 86/20, 83/46, 63/149(6), see 1989/78 & 90B/260(2)

DISTRIBUTION OF PROFITS

assurance company and, 83/48, see 1989/78 & 90B/260(2)
investment company and, 83/47, see 1989/78 & 90B/260(2)
investment company, alternative basis for calculating permitted distribution, 83/47, see 1989/78
meaning of, 83/51, see 1989/78
"profits available for distribution"
-payment out of, 83/45, see 1989/78
-rules for calculating, 83/45, see 1989/78
public limited company, additional condition to be satisfied, 83/46, see 1989/78
realised losses, and, 83/45, see 1989/78
realised profits, and, 83/45, see 1989/78
"relevant accounts" under Act of 1983, 83/49, see 1989/78
restrictions on, 83/51, see 1989/78
restrictions on public limited companies, 83/45-51, see 1989/78
unlawful, consequences of, 83/50, see 1989/78

DIVIDENDS

conditions for payment, [see **Distributions**]
fixed cumulative, details of any arrears to be given in accounts, 86/4(15), S25 & 37
payment in proportion to amount paid up on shares, 63/66
unclaimed, on a winding up, 63/307

DOCUMENTS

annexed to accounts, meaning, 63/164
company of, how authenticated, 63/42
destruction of or mutilation of, 90B/243
directors' names to be stated on, what, 63/196
dissolved company, relating to, disposal of by registrar, 63/313
false statements in certain, penalty for making, 90B/242 (63/380 repealed by 90B/6), (63/X repealed by 90B/6)
fees payable to registrar for inspection, 63/370
inspection of, kept by registrar, 63/370
meaning of, 63/2(1), 90B/3
Minister of, how authenticated, 63/394
Minister's power to require production, 90B/19
name of company, required on what, 63/114
offer of shares or debentures to public, containing, deemed a prospectus, 63/51
production of, to examiner, 90/8-AM 90B/180
production of, to inspectors, 90B/10 & 17
registrar
-enforcement of duty to deliver to, 63/371
-inspection and copies of, 63/370
-kept by, evidence of, 63/370(3)
sealing of, by registrar, 63/368
service on company, 63/379(1)

EMOLUMENTS

directors', particulars of, to be given in accounts, 63/191, see 86/S49
-aggregate amounts to be shown in profit and loss account, 86/S49
-prohibition of tax-free payments, 63/185
employees', details in accounts, 86/S42

EMPLOYEES

particulars in accounts, 86/S42

EMPLOYEES' SHARE SCHEME

allotment of shares under, authorisation of directors not required, 83/23, see 1989/78 & 90B/260(2)
allotment of shares under, pre-emption rights not applicable on, 83/23, see 1989/78 & 90B/260(2)
financial assistance for, 63/60(13), see 1989/78 & 90B/260(1) & 155 & 224
meaning, 83/2(1)
offer of shares or debentures to be allotted under, presumed not "to public", 63/61-AM 90B/238, see 83/21(2)
pre-emption rights of holders under scheme, 83/23, see 1989/78 & 90B/260(2)
re-registration of private company, share capital rules, 83/10
residual interests under, 83/42 & 43

ENTERPRISES

meaning of, 78/1

EQUITABLE MORTGAGE

land, of, registration of charges, and, 63/99

EQUITY SECURITIES

meaning of, 63/155(5), 83/2(1), 83/23(13), see 1989/78

EVIDENCE

books of company to be, on winding up, 63/304
statements made to inspectors, when admissible as, 90B/18

EXAMINATION

officers of company and other persons, of, 90B/126 (replacing 63/245), see 90B/251

EXAMINER

agent, as, 90/7(7)
appointment
-application for, 90/2
.insurer, may only be made by Minister, 90/3(2)
.licensed bank, may only be made by Central Bank of Ireland, 90/3(2)
.precluded if receiver has stood appointed for three days prior to presentation, 90/3(6)-AM 90B/180
.security for costs required, 90/3(5)
-by court, 90/2
-ceases on cessation of protection of court, 90/26
-order of, examiner to deliver copy to registrar within three days after appointment, 90/12(3)
-petition for, petitioner to deliver copy to registrar within three days of presentation, 90/12(1)
auditor, extension of powers of, to, 90/7(1)
charged property, power to deal with, 90/11-AM 90B/181
compromise, [see **Scheme of arrangement** below]
costs of, 90/29
court
-Circuit Court, may be remitted to, 90/3(9)
-further powers of, 90/9

continued

Examiner continued
-may apply for direction to, 90/7(6)
-may decide on private hearings, 90/31
-may enforce court orders made outside the State, 90/36
-may impose other duties, 90/15(2)
creditors' committee
-court may direct appointment of, 90/21(1)
-examiner may appoint, 90/21(1)
-examiner to meet, 90/21(4)
-membership of, 90/21(2)
-opinion of, 90/21(3)
detrimental acts etc., power to halt etc., 90/7(5)
directors' duty to submit statement of affairs to, within seven days of appointment, 90/14(1)
directors' meeting
-entitled to notice of and to attend, 90/7(3)
-powers of control, 90/7(2)
directors' powers
-may be restricted by court, 90/3(8)
-may be exercisable by examiner only, 90/9(1)
employees, 90/9(2)
examination of affairs of company, 90/15(1)
examine under oath, power to, 90/8(4)
general meetings
-entitled to notice of and to attend, 90/7(3)
-powers of control, 90/7(2)
hearings, right to appear and be heard, 90/17(2)
"interested party", 90/1
liabilities of, 90/10-AM 90B/180
management of company, control over, 90/7(5)
nomination of, 90/3(3)
-written consent of nominated person required, 90/3(4)
orders, delivery of copies to registrar, 90/17(5)
-notice of delivery to be published in "Iris Oifigiuil" within fourteen days, 90/30-AM 90B/181
performance of, determination of questions arising, 90/13(7)
period of three months from appointment
-attachment etc. prohibited, 90/5(2)-AM 90B/180
continued

Examiner continued
-bank accounts may not be set off without examiner's consent, 90/5(2)-AM 90B/180
-charge may not be realised, 90/5(2)-AM 90B/180
-goods on hire purchase may not be re-possessed, 90/5(2)-AM 90B/180 & 181
-order under 63/205 may not be made, 90/5(2)-AM 90B/180
-restriction on receiver, 90/5(2)-AM 90B/180 & 181
-winding up may not commence, 90/5(2)-AM 90B/180
persons disqualified from acting as, 90/28
powers of, 90/7
protection of court, cessation
-on commencement of scheme of arrangement, 90/26
-on expiry of three months from date of appointment of examiner, 90/26
-on such earlier date as court may direct, 90/26
protection of court, extension of, 90/18(4)
protection of court, petition for, 90/3
-effect on creditors and others, 90/5-AM 90B/180
-existence of receiver for three days precludes, 90/3(6)-AM 90B/180
provisional liquidator, effect on, 90/6
publication of appointment, 90/12(2)
qualifications of, 90/28
receiver, effect on, 90/6
related companies, 90/4-AM 90B/181
removal of, 90/13(1)
remuneration of, 90/29
reports
-examiner to supply copies to company and interested parties, 90/15(3 & 4)
-hearing of matters arising, 90/17
.court may make order after hearing, 90/17(3)
-initial examination of, within twenty-one days of appointment, 90/15(1)
.contents of, 90/16-AM 90B/180
resignation of, 90/13(1)
scheme of arrangement
-acceptance of

continued

Examiner continued
.by members, 90/23(3)
.by creditors, 90/23(4)
-contents of, 90/22
-consideration of, by members and/or creditors, 90/23
-court
.decisions, challenge of, 90/25
.effect of an approval, 90/24-AM 90B/180
.may confirm, modify or refuse, 90/24(3)-AM 90B/180(3)
.notice of delivery of copy order to registrar to be published in "Iris Oifigiuil", 90/30-AM 90B/181
.objection, creditor or member may make, 90/25
.order, examiner to deliver copy to registrar, 90/24(10)-AM 90B/180
.persons who may attend and be heard, 90/24(2)-AM 90B/180
.to consider as soon as possible, 90/24(1)-AM 90B/180
-creditors' interests, impairment of, 90/22(5)
-implementation and supervision of, 90/24(8)-AM 90B/180
-meetings, summoning and decisions of, 90/23
-members' interests, impairment of, 90/22(6)
-modification of, examiner may refuse, 90/23(2)
-proposals for, 90/18 & 19
-publication of confirmed proposal in "Iris Oifigiuil", 90/30-AM 90B/181
-revocation on grounds of fraud, 90/27
-repudiation of contracts under, 90/20
-stationery to bear statement "under the protection of the court", 90/12(4)
vacancy, filled by court, 90/13(2)
winding up
-application of certain provisions to, 90B/138(8) (90/33(9) repealed by 90B/180)
-court may order, 90/17(4)
-date of commencement, 90/17(6)

EXECUTION

against company, when creditor not entitled to benefit, 63/291

continued

Execution continued
-liquidator's right in respect of goods taken in, 63/292
-void in winding up by the court, 63/219
members of company not formed under Act, not to issue against, 63/339

EXPERT

prospectus containing statement by, consent required, 63/46-AM 82/I
report by, required before allotment of shares in public limited company, where consideration not in cash, 83/30, see 1989/78
right of, to be indemnified by directors, when, 63/49(6)
statement by
-in case of foreign company, 63/363
-liability of, for untrue, 63/49(2)
-provisions when prospectus contains, 63/46
-untrue, ground of defence, when, 63/49(3)

EXTRAORDINARY GENERAL MEETING

[see **General meeting**]
auditor, right to requisition if resigning, 90B/186
members, called by, 63/132, 63/134
power of court to convene, 63/135
serious loss of capital, to be called on, 83/40, see 1989/78 & 90B/260(2)

FALSE INFORMATION

[see **Investigations**]
furnishing of, 90B/242

FALSE STATEMENTS

in balance sheet and certain other documents, penalty for, 90B/242 (63/380 repealed by 90B/6)
in prospectus, 90B/243 (63/X repealed by 90B/6) [see **Prospectus**]

FALSIFICATION OF BOOKS ETC.

by officer, an offence, 90B/243

FEES

inspectors' report, for copy of, 90B/11(3)
payable to registrar, provisions as to, 63/369, 63/VIII
-Minister may alter, 63/395(2)

FILING REQUIREMENTS

allotment of shares, where consideration given, 63/58-AM 82/19-AM 82/I, see 83/31(2) & 55(1g)
annual return, 63/125-AM 90B/244, see 90B/260
accounts, [see **Accounts**]
auditor, removal of, 90B/183
auditor's statement of resignation, 90B/185(3)
capital, increase of, 63/70, see 1989/78 & 90B/260(1)
charge created, 63/99-AM 90B/122, 63/100
charge existing on acquired property, 63/101
charge, satisfaction and release of, 63/105
commission, where shares not offered to public, 63/59
conversion of shares etc., 63/69, see 1989/78 & 90B/221 & 260(1)
debenture holders, register of, where kept, 63/116(7)
director, first and change of, 90B/51(6) (replacing 63/195(6)-AM 82/8), 82/3
directors' interests in shares, 90B/60(6)
directors, register of, change in, 90B/51 (replacing 63/195)
directors' service contract, where kept, 90B/50(4)
enforcement of duty to make returns, 63/371
expert's report, non-cash allotment, 83/31, see 1989/78
members, register of, 63/116(7)
memorandum, alteration of objects, 1973/163/5
prospectus, copies of, 63/47-AM 82/I
registered office, change in, 63/113(2)-AM 82/4
resolutions, special or ordinary, 63/143-AM 82/5-AM 82/I-AM 83/I

continued

Filing requirements continued
satisfaction or release of charge, 63/105
secretary, first and change of, 90B/51 (replacing 63/195(6)-AM 82/8), 82/3
shares purchase of own, 63/60, see 1989/78 & 90B/260(1) & 155 & 224
shares, special rights attaching, 83/39

FINANCIAL ASSISTANCE BY COMPANY FOR ACQUISITION OF ITS SHARES

[see **Acquisition by Company of Its Own Shares; Capital redemption reserve; Purchase by company of its own shares**]
disclosure of aggregate of outstanding loans in balance sheet, 86/S37
employee share schemes, exception for, 63/60(13), see 1989/78 & 90B/260(1) & 155 & 224
general prohibition, 63/60, see 1989/78 & 90B/260(1) & 155 & 224 & 86/S37(2)
holding company's shares, extension of prohibition to, 63/60, see 1989/78 & 90B/260(1) & 155 & 224
private company, power to give financial assistance in certain cases, 63/60, see 1989/78 & 90B/260(1) & 155 & 224

FINANCIAL YEAR

meaning of, 63/2(1), 63/IIIpIII/28, see 90B/221
subsidiaries of, provisions as to, 63/153

FINES

application of, 63/386
daily default fines, 90B/240(6)

FIXED ASSETS

alternative accounting rules and, 86/S17-22
historical cost accounting rules and, 86/S4-16
continued

Fixed assets continued
meaning, 86/S60
meaning, for calculating permitted distribution, 86/S60

FLOATING CHARGE

appointment of receiver to enforce, provisions applicable on, 63/319 & 320
invalid, time limits, 90B/136 (replacing 63/288), 63/289
preferential payments, when possession taken of property subject to, 63/98
-in winding up to have priority notwithstanding, 63/285(7)-AM 90B/134
receiver appointed under, payment of preferential creditors by, 63/98
registered land, and, registration, and, 63/99
registration of, 63/99-AM 90B/122
time limit for creation, 90B/136 (replacing 63/288)
void in winding up when, 90B/136 (replacing 63/288), 63/289
winding up by court, and, 90B/136 (replacing 63/288)

FLOTATION OF COMPANY

[see **Prospectus**]
compliance in practice with requirements of stock exchange, 1984/282, see 1991/18
European Communities (Stock Exchange) Regulations 1984, [see **Stock Exchange**]
legal controls on, 63/44-52, 63/III, see 90B/221, 1984/282, see 1991/18
misleading statements made in connection with, civil liability for, 63/49
mis-statements in connection with, criminal liability for, 63/50-AM 82/I
quotation for shares, 1984/282, see 1991/18
recognised stock exchange, and, 1984/282, see 1991/18

FOREIGN COMPANY

accounts of, 63/354
application for shares of, and debentures in,
provisions as to, 63/361(4)
ceasing to carry on business in the State, notice to be
given to the registrar, 63/357
charge on property of, registration of, 63/111
documents of, to be delivered to registrar by,
63/352-354
-alterations in, return as to, to registrar, 63/353
interpretation of, provisions as to, 63/359 & 360
investigation of, Minister's powers, 90B/17
meaning of, and provisions applicable to, 63/351
name of, obligations as to, 63/355
offences in relation to, penalty for, 63/358-AM 82/I
prospectus of
-meaning of, 63/367(4)
-mis-statement in, civil liability for, 63/366
-provisions as to, 63/355 & 361
-penalty for contravening, 63/365
-relaxation of in certain cases, 63/362
-registration of, and documents to be attached to,
63/364
-statement of expert in, provisions where, 63/363
service on, how effected, 63/356
shares or debentures of, meaning of, 63/367(4)

FOREIGN LANGUAGES

contracts in, referred to in prospectus, 63/47(1)
-in case of foreign company, 63/364(2)
documents annexed to annual return, in, 63/128(1)

FORFEITURE OF SHARES

reduction of capital, and, 63/72-AM 90B/231, see
1989/78 & 90B/260(1)
re-registration, and, 83/43

FORMATION OF COMPANIES

[see **Articles of association; Memorandum of association; Name of company**]
documents to be delivered to registrar, 63/17, 82/3
guarantee company, 63/11-AM 82/2, 63/12-AM 82/l, 63/16-AM 82/17
official notification, 1973/163
payment of capital duty, Finance Act 1973/69-71
public company, 63/5
registration fee, amount of, 63/369
re-registration of private company as public, 83/9
re-registration of public company as private, 83/14
statutory declaration as to compliance with Acts, 83/6, see 1989/78 & 90B/256, (63/19 repealed 83/l)
unlimited company, 63/6-AM 83/l & 11-AM 82/2 & 12-82/l & 16-AM 82/17, see 1989/78
unregistered company, [see **Unregistered company**]

FORMS

[see **Appendix**]

FRAUD

investigation, may be ground for, 90B/8 (replacing 63/166)
modification of principle in Saloman's case, and, 90B/137 (replacing 63/297), 90B/138, see 90B/251
officers of company subsequently wound up, of, 63/295, see 90B/251
person guilty of, may be prohibited from being a director, 90B/160 (63/184 repealed by 90B/6)
shares allotted for consideration other than cash, and, 63/58, 83/26 & 29-34

FRAUDULENT PREFERENCE

acts prior to winding up, deemed to be, 90B/135 (replacing 63/286-AM Second Schedule, Bankruptcy Act, 1988)

continued

Fraudulent preference continued
liabilities and rights of persons preferred, 63/287
meaning and effect of, 90B/135 (replacing 63/286-AM Second Schedule, Bankruptcy Act, 1988)
mortgage or charge, and, 63/287
third party proceedings in respect of, 63/287(3)

FRAUDULENT TRADING

not limited to directors, 90B/137 (replacing 63/297), 90B/138, see 90B/251
provisions as to civil and criminal liability for, 90B/137 (replacing 63/297), 90B/138, see 90B/251
responsibility on directors, 90B/137 (replacing 63/297), 90B/138, see 90B/251

GENERAL MEETING

Accounts, [see **Accounts**]
adjourned, resolution passed at, date of, 63/144, see 90/23(6)
annual, [see **Annual General meeting**]
auditor entitled to receive notice of, to attend and be heard at, 90B/193(5) (63/163 repealed by 90B/6)
auditors, appointment and removal of, at, 63/160-AM 90B/183, 63/161-AM 90B/184
calling of, requirements as to, 63/134, see 83/38(6)
capital, on serious loss of, 83/40, see 1989/78 & 90B/260(2)
copies of balance sheet etc. to members before, 63/159
corporations acting by representatives at, 63/139
court may order, to be called, 63/135
extraordinary, may be requisitioned, 63/132 [see **Extraordinary general meeting**]
general provisions as to, where none in articles, 63/134
Minister may direct calling of, when, 63/131(3)
minute books, form of, 63/378
minute books, inspection, 63/146, see 90B/105

continued

General meeting continued
minutes of, to be kept, 63/145, see 90B/27(3)
notice for, who must be given, 63/134
notice of, length of, 63/133
-extended, 63/142
-short, when, may be held on, 63/133(3)
one person may constitute, when, 63/131(3) & 135(1)
poll at, provisions as to demand of, 63/137
proxies at, provisions as to, 63/136
resolution passed at adjournment, deemed date of, 63/144, see 90/23(6)
resolution, extended notice of, period of notice required, 63/142
resolutions passed at, types which must be forwarded to registrar, 63/143-AM 82/5-AM 82/I-AM 83/I, see 83/18(6) & 39 & 53(1) & 55(1g)
voluntary winding up
-creditors
.final, liquidator to call in, when, 63/273
.liquidator to call in, when, 63/272-AM 90B/145
-members
.final, liquidator to call in, when, 63/263
.liquidator to call in, when, 63/262-AM 90B/145
.liquidator's power to summon, in, 63/276, see 90B/131
votes at, entitlement to, 63/134, see 83/38(6)

GOODWILL

accounts, in, 86/S9 & 51, note 2 balance sheet format
charge on, requires registration, 63/99

GOING CONCERN - ACCOUNTING PRINCIPLES

requirement, 86/5

GROUP ACCOUNTS

[see **Accounts**]
auditors to report on, 90B/193(1) (63/163 repealed by 90B/6)

continued

Group accounts continued
balance sheet, to be annexed to, 63/157
-may be incorporated in, 63/151(3)
consolidated accounts, to be, 63/151
-provisions as to, 63/VIpII
contents of, 63/152
duty of holding company to prepare, lay and deliver, 63/150-AM 82/I, see 86/S76 & 90B/41 & 43
exemption from requirements, 63/151
failure by director to secure compliance as to, 63/153-AM 82/I, 63/150-AM 82/I, see 90B/41 & 43
"fellow subsidiary", 86/S63
financial year of holding company and subsidiary, 63/153-AM 82/I
foreign company, of, 63/354
form of, 63/151
"group company", 86/S64
holding companies and, subsidiaries, 63/155
holding company, definition of, 63/155
private company as holding company, and, 63/154
provisions applying to, 86/3 & S45-55
subsidiary, definition of, 63/155
when required, 63/150, see 90B/41 & 43
where not submitted, provisions, applicable, 63/VIpII/15(4)

GUARANTEE

company limited by, [see **Company Limited By Guarantee**]
notes to accounts, details in, 86/S36

GUARANTOR

fraudulent preference of, 63/287(3)

HISTORICAL COST CONVENTION

accounts, rules applying to, 86/S4-16

HOLDING COMPANY

[see **Group accounts; Subsidiary**]
accounts of, exemption from requirements, 63/150, see 90B/41 & 43
duty to ensure that financial year coincides with that of subsidiary, 63/153-AM 82/I
private company as, group accounts, and, 63/154
what is, 63/155

INCOME AND EXPENDITURE ACCOUNT

reference to profit and loss account includes references to, 63/149(8)
to be laid before company in general meeting, when, 63/148, see 83/49 & 86/3 & 90B/43

INCOME TAX

payments to directors may not be free of, 63/185

INCORPORATION

meaning and mode of, 63/5
outside the State, [see **Foreign company**]

INDEMNITY

to officers and auditors against liability, when void, 63/200-AM 83/I

INDEX

how to be kept, 63/378
kept by company, form of, 63/378

INDEX OF MEMBERS

company to keep, 63/117
inspection of, 63/119-AM 82/I, 63/120, see 90B/105 & 260
when required, 63/117

INDUSTRIAL & PROVIDENT SOCIETIES

auditor, persons disqualified from being, 90B/187 (82/6(6) repealed by 90B/6)
winding up, application of Act to, Industrial & Provident Societies (Amendment) Act, 1978/19

INSIDER DEALINGS

business relationship, 90B/108(11)
communication of information by individual, 90B/108(5)
"dealing", 90B/107
dealing, restriction on, 90B/112
dealings on stock exchange on the basis of inside information, prohibition, 90B/108
defences, 90B/108 & 110
"director", 90B/107
exempt transaction, 90B/110
"individual connected with a company", 90B/108(11)
information obtained by person in public office, prohibition on abuse, 90B/108
"officer", 90B/107
options dealings, director etc., 90B/30
penalties, 90B/114
professional relationship, 90B/108(11)
"public office", 90B/107
recognised stock exchange
-annual report of, 90B/120
-application of, 1984/282, see 1991/18, 90B/119
-authorised person, 90B/117
.duty of relevant authority to ensure avoidance of potential conflict of interest, 90B/117(2)

continued

Insider dealings continued
-co-operation with other authorities outside the State, 90B/116
-duty in relation to unlawful dealing, 90B/115
-meaning, 90B/107
-Minister's powers to make supplementary regulations, 90B/121
-obligation of professional secrecy, 90B/118
-relevant authority, 90B/107
-"related company", 90B/107
"securities", 90B/107
stock exchange, dealings on, prohibitions, 90B/108(5)
transactions prohibited, 90B/108
trustees and personal representatives, 90B/110
"underwrite", 90B/107
unlawful dealing
-agent's duty in relation to, 90B/113
-civil liability for, 90B/109
-criminal liability for, 90B/111
unpublished price-sensitive information, 90B/108(2)

INSOLVENT COMPANIES

disqualification of directors of, 90B/150

INSPECTION OF BOOKS

[see **Minister; Investigations**]
destruction, mutilation etc. of books, an offence, 90B/243
documents etc., production to Minister, 90B/19
entry and search of premises for purposes of, 90B/20
privileged information on, 90B/23
security of information received, restrictions on disclosure, 90B/21

INSURANCE COMPANIES

directors of, proposal to appoint must be submitted to Minister for approval, s 20 Insurance Act, 1989
distributions by, alternative means of calculating permitted distribution, 83/47, see 1989/78 & 90B/260(2)

INTERESTS IN SHARES

[see **Directors' interests in shares etc.; Disclosure of interests in shares of public limited company; Investigation by public company of interests in its own shares**]

INVESTIGATIONS

circumstances in which initiated, 90B/7 (replacing 63/165)
conduct of, 90B/9 (replacing 63/167), 90B/10 (replacing 63/168-AM 82/7)
court may give directions to ensure investigation is carried out as quickly and inexpensively as possible, 90B/7(4)
court may provide for, on application of members, 90B/7 (replacing 63/165)
documents, Minister's power to require production, 90B/19
evidence, taking of, and production of documents in, 90B/10 (replacing 63/168-AM 82/7)
examination of officers of company on oath, 90B/10(4) (replacing 63/168(2))
examiner, production of documents and evidence to, 90/8-AM 90B/180
expenses of, 90B/13 (replacing 63/171)
extended to other bodies corporate, when may be, 90B/9 (replacing 63/167)
foreign companies, application to, 90B/17
in other cases when, 90B/8 (replacing 63/166)
inspector appointed for, under 1908 Act, 63/3(3)
inspectors
-appointment to investigate company's affairs
.application for, 90B/7
.application of Minister for, 90B/8
.on court order, 90B/7
-directors' share interests etc., appointment to investigate, 90B/66

continued

Investigations continued
-ownership of company, appointment to investigate, 90B/14
-power to inform court of offence, 90B/11(2)
-procedures to be followed by, 90B/9 & 10 (replacing 63/167 & 168-AM 82/7)
-production of documents and evidence to, 90B/10
-related companies, power to investigate, 90B/9
inspectors' reports
-evidence of inspectors' opinions, admissible as, 90B/22
-obligation to make and disclosure of, 90B/11 (replacing 63/169)
-power of Minister to present petition for winding up following receipt of, 90B/12(2)
-remedying any disability suffered by any person, court may order after consideration, 90B/12
-winding up, court may order after consideration of, 90B/12(1)
Minister's power to require information about share interests and to impose restrictions, 90B/15-16
ownership of company, of, 90B/14-16
privileged information, and, 90B/23 (replacing 63/173)
proceedings for damages after, 90B/12 (replacing 63/170)
production of company books and documents, 90B/10 (replacing 63/168-AM 82/7)
referral of matter to Director of Public Prosecutions, (63/170 repealed 90B/6)
regulations, Minister's power to make supplementary, 90B/24
report of, provisions as to, 90B/11 (replacing 63/169)
-proceedings on, 90B/12 (replacing 63/170)
-what matters, evidence of, 90B/22 (replacing 63/172)
search of premises, 90B/20
shares and debentures, of interests in, 90B/15 [see **Disclosure of interests in shares of public limited company**]
shares and debentures, of directors' interests and dealings in, 90B/66 [see **Directors' interests in shares etc.**]

INVESTIGATION BY PUBLIC LIMITED COMPANY OF INTERESTS IN ITS SHARES

[see **Disclosure of interests in shares of public limited company; Register of interests in shares**]
information on interest in its shares, power of public company to require, 90B/81
interest in shares, 90B/81
investigation and report on requisition of members, 90B/82-84
offence of failure to provide required information, 90B/85
recognised stock exchange
-annual report of, 90B/93
-co-operation between Member States, 90B/96
-duty to notify certain interests, 90B/91 & 93
.duty of relevant authority to report contravention to Director of Public Prosecutions, 90B/92
-immunity from suit, 90B/95
-interpretation, 90B/90
-obligation of professional secrecy, 90B/94
registration of information received, in company's register of interests in shares, 90B/82
-removal of entries, 90B/86
.when entries not to be removed, 90B/87
"relevant share capital", 90B/67(2)
restrictions on shares, power when information refused, 90B/16, see 90B/85

INVESTMENT COMPANY

accounts of, special provisions for, 86/3 & S56-59
distribution of profits, and, 83/47, see 1989/78 & 90B/260(2)
meaning of, 83/47, see 1989/78 & 90B/260(2)

INVESTMENT COMPANIES (UCITS)

Central Bank of Ireland
-authorisation to carry on business, by, 90B/256

continued

Investment companies continued
-powers of, 90B/257
Companies Acts, restriction of certain provisions of, 90B/260
default of, or failure in performance of its investments, 90B/259
"investment company", 90B/252
Minister may make supplementary regulations, 90B/261
offences under, 90B/252-262,
own shares, power of investment company to purchase, 90B/254
"property", 90B/252
purchased shares, treatment of, 90B/255
share capital of, 90B/253
"UCITS Regulations", 90B/252
-adaptation of certain provisions, 90B/258

INVOICES

of company, in liquidation, to state fact, 63/303
-when receiver appointed, to state fact, 63/317
records of receipts and expenditure to be kept, 90B/202

IRREDEEMABLE DEBENTURES

provisions as to, 63/94

"IRIS OIFIGIUIL"

examiner, notice of delivery of court orders to registrar to be published within fourteen days, 90/30-AM 90B/181
liquidator, publication of appointment of, within twenty-one days, 63/227
notice of certain matters to be published by public limited companies, 83/55, see 90B/221
publication by company of notification of receipt and issue of certain documents, 1973/163/4
winding up, resolution for voluntary, to be published, 63/252-AM 82/I

JOINT STOCK BANKS

enactments, relating to not repealed, 63/XIII

JOINT STOCK COMPANY

definition of, for purposes of registration under Act, 63/329, see 83/18(1) & 37(1c)
company formed or registered under Joint Stock Companies Acts etc., application of Companies Acts to, 63/324
company registered under Joint Stock Companies Acts etc., provisions relating to share capital, 63/330
registration under Part VIII as a company limited by shares, 63/330-AM 83/I
name, requirements as to, 63/334
requirements for registration of, under Act, 63/330

JOINT STOCK COMPANIES ACTS

company, existing, includes companies formed and registered under, 63/2(1)
-registered, but not formed under, 63/325
-registered under, transfer of shares of, 63/327(1)
meaning of, 63/2(1)
unlimited company under, alterations to capital of, 63/327(2)

JUDGE

[see **Court**]
application to, for production and inspection of books or papers, 63/384

JUDGEMENT MORTGAGE

registration of, 63/102

"JUST AND EQUITABLE"

grounds for winding up, 63/213

LAND

charge on, requires registration, 63/99
effect of provisions of former Companies Acts, 63/108

LEASEHOLD PROPERTY

disclaimer of, in winding up, 63/290(8)
winding up of company, and, 63/290(8)

LEGAL PROCEEDINGS

[see **Court**]
costs, 63/390
disclosure of documents, 90B/19
disqualification orders, 90B/160 (63/184-AM 82/I repealed by 90B/6)
duty to make returns, enforcement, 63/371
provisions relating to, 63/390 & 391
relief, 63/391

LETTERS OF ADMINISTRATION

evidence of, 63/87(2)

LIABILITIES

how to be shown in accounts, 63/VIpl

LIABILITY

members of, limited, to be stated in memorandum, 63/6, see 1989/78
-extent of, 63/18(2)

"LICENSED BANK"

meaning, for provisions relating to loans etc., 90B/25(1)

LIEN

public limited company cannot create charges over its own shares, 83/44
unenforceability of, on books etc., by liquidator or examiner, 90B/125 (90/32 repealed by 90B/180), see 90B/180(2A)

"LIMITED"

[see **Name of company**]
company exempt from requirements to include in name, 63/24, 83/58
disclosure of limited liability in business letters etc., 1973/163/9
name of company to end with, 63/6-AM 83/I, see 1989/78
penalty for improper use, 63/381-AM 82/I

LIMITED COMPANY

conversion into unlimited company, 83/52
conversion of unlimited company into, 83/53 (63/20 cesser 83/53)

LIMITED PARTNERSHIP

winding up of, provisions of Act to apply to, (63/345(8) repealed by Second Schedule, Bankruptcy Act, 1988)

LIQUIDATION

voluntary, reconstruction by, 63/260, see 1987/137

LIQUIDATOR (ALL MODES) 63/206-211 & 283-312

application to prevent person from being a director, to appear on, 90B/160 (63/184 repealed by 90B/6)
Bank of Ireland, payment into by, 63/307
body corporate may not be, 63/300

continued

Liquidator (all modes) continued
books and papers of, when prima facie evidence, 63/304
corrupt inducement given for purpose of affecting appointment of, 63/301
court power to assess damages against directors, extension of, 90B/148
creditor's representative, duty to disclose connection to proposed liquidator, 90B/147
disclaim onerous property etc., when may, 63/290
disqualification for appointment as, 63/300-AM 82/I, 90B/146
enforcement of duties of, 63/302
execution, right of, as to goods, taken in, 63/292
meetings of contributories summoned by, 63/309
misfeasance proceedings, and, 90B/142 (replacing 63/298), see 90B/251
notice of appointment, 63/278-AM 82/I, see 82/16
notification on invoices, letters etc. that company in liquidation, 63/303-AM 82/I
offence disclosed to, duties of, as to, 63/299-AM 90B/143, see 90B/179
position of, 90B/142 (replacing 63/298), see 90B/251
powers of, 63/260 & 290, see 1987/137
qualifications of, Minister's powers to amend by regulations, 90B/237
receiver, remuneration of, may apply to court to fix, 63/318
-where same person as, 63/319(5)
registrar, information to be given to by, when winding up not completed within two years, 63/306-AM 82/I-AM 90B/145
returns, court may enforce duty of, to make, 63/302
returns, penalty for default in making, 90B/145
-duty to report whether any officer director or member is the subject of a declaration of personal liability for all or any part of debts of company or is subject or deemed to be subject to disqualification order, 90B/144
shares etc., as consideration for property, acceptance of, 63/260 & 271, see 83/30(14a) & 1987/137

LIQUIDATOR (WINDING UP, COURT, BY) 63/215-250
account of, order for payment of monies to, 63/239
appointment of, 63/225
appointment of, publication in "Iris Oifigiuil" of, within twenty-one days, 63/227
committee of inspection, and, 63/232 & 233
company's property, custody of and vesting in, winding up by court, 63/229 & 230
company's property, delivery to, on winding up order, 63/236
contributories, and, [see **Contributories**]
declaration of dividends by, Rules Or74 r118, 119, and 121-124
dissolution of company, application to court for, 63/249-AM 82/I
duties of, 63/229
file of proceedings, Rules Or74 r133
more than one, 63/228
meetings of creditors or contributories, when to be summoned by, 63/232(1)
order for payment or delivery of property to, 90B/127
payment in of money by, Rules Or74 r118 & 119
powers of, 63/231-AM 90B/124
-application to court as to exercise of, 63/231(3)
property of company, court may require to be delivered to, 63/236
-to take custody of, 63/229
-vesting of, in, order for, 63/230
provisional, Rules Or74 r15, [see **Provisional liquidator**]
remuneration of, 63/228, Rules Or74 r47
resignation or removal of, 63/228
sales of property by, Rules Or74 r125, Or51
-costs of, 63/281
security to be given by, 63/228
style of, 63/228
vacancy in office of, how filled, 63/228
validity of acts of, 63/228

LIQUIDATOR (WINDING UP, VOLUNTARY, BOTH KINDS) 63/251-282

appointment of
-notification to, 90B/133
-prior written consent required, 90B/133
application to court by, 63/280, see 90B/131
appointment and removal of by court, 63/277
notice of appointment of, to registrar required within fourteen days, 63/278
powers and duties of, 63/276, see 90B/131
remuneration of, payable in priority to other claims, 63/281

LIQUIDATOR (WINDING UP, VOLUNTARY, CREDITORS) 63/265-273

appointment of, 63/267
meetings to be called by, 63/272-AM 82/I-AM 90B/145, 63/273-AM 82/I, see 82/16
remuneration of, how fixed, 63/269(1)
sale, power of, to accept shares etc., in purchasing company on, 63/271
style and title of, 63/228
vacancy in office of, 63/270

LIQUIDATOR (WINDING UP, VOLUNTARY, MEMBERS) 63/257-264

appointment of, 63/258
creditors, when to summon meeting of, 90B/129 (replacing 63/261)
general meeting, when to call, 63/262-AM 82/I-AM 90B/145, 63/263-AM 82/I, 63/276, see 90B/131
opinion of, that company unable to pay its debts in time stated in statutory declaration, effect of, 90B/129 (replacing 63/261), 63/264
remuneration of, 63/258
sale, power of, to accept shares etc., in purchasing company, on, 63/260, see 1987/137
vacancy in office of, 63/259

LISTING PARTICULARS

contents of, 1984/282, see 1991/18
delivery to registrar, 1984/282, see 1991/18
offences in connection with, 1984/282, see 1991/18
persons responsible for providing information,
    1984/282, see 1991/18

LOANS ETC. TO DIRECTORS AND CONNECTED PERSONS

amount, when small, 90B/32
business transaction, 90B/37
"connected person", 90B/26
contracts of employment, 90B/28
"credit transaction", 90B/25(1)
criminal offence, breach of prohibitions, 90B/40
disclosure of, in accounts, 90B/41-44 (63/192 cesser
    90B/49)
-auditors' duty, in breach of, 90B/46
-exclusions, 90B/45
exceptions to the prohibitions, 90B/32-37
expenditure on company duty, funds for, 90B/36
financial limits, power of Minister to alter, 90B/48
groups, between companies in, 90B/34
"guarantee", 90B/25(1)
holding company, transaction with, 90B/35
indemnity, 90B/25(1)
"licensed bank", 90B/25(1)
licensed bank, further provisions, 90B/44
limits, financial, alteration of, 90B/48
minor transactions, 90B/32
options, 90B/30
particulars in accounts of loans, 90B/41-43
personal liability for company debts in certain cases,
    90B/39
prohibitions applying to all companies, 90B/31
property transactions, 90B/29
"quasi-loan", 90B/25(1)
relevant assets, 90B/29(2)

continued

Loans etc. to directors and connected persons continued
-reduction in amount of, 90B/33
"relevant period" for purposes of, 90B/41 & 43 & 45, 90B/41(9)
remedies for breach of provisions, civil, 90B/38
"shadow director", 90B/27
transactions, 90B/25
unregistered companies, application of disclosure provisions to, 90B/S
value, of transactions and arrangements, 90B/25(4)

MAINTENANCE OF CAPITAL

acquisition by a company of its own shares, (63/64 cesser 90B/220) [see **Shares**]
extraordinary general meeting, and, 83/40, see 1989/78 & 90B/260(2)
meeting to consider serious loss of capital, 83/40, see 90B/260(2)
reduction sanctioned by court, 63/72-AM 90B/231(1), see 83/17(1) & 38(3c) & 43(3) & 55(1i) & 1989/78 & 90B/260(1)

MANAGEMENT OF COMPANY

disqualification of persons from [see **Disqualification order**]

MANAGER

[see **Officer; Receiver**]

MANAGING DIRECTOR

service contract of, 63/182

MEDIUM SIZED COMPANIES

[see entry under **Accounts**]

MEETINGS

[see **Annual general meetings; Creditors; Directors; Extraordinary general meeting; General meeting; Poll; Proxy; Quorum; Winding up, (all modes)**]
class of, [see **Class]**
compromise or arrangement, in connection, with, notice of, 63/202-AM 82/I, see 1987/137 & 90/23(7)
-order for, 63/201-AM 82/I, see 1987/137
corporation, how represented at, 63/139
in creditors' voluntary winding up, company to summon, of creditors, 63/266-AM 82/I-AM 90B/130, see 90B/131
-liquidator to summon, of creditors, at end of each year, 63/272-AM 82/I-AM 90B/145, see 82/16
-liquidator to summon final, of creditors, when, 63/273-AM 82/I, see 82/16
in members' voluntary winding up, of creditors, when to be summoned, 90B/129 (replacing 63/261-AM 82/I)
-separate, to consider appointment of committee of inspection, 63/232
in winding up of all kinds, court may direct, 63/309
-creditors and contributories of, adjourned, 63/308
minutes of, 63/145(3), see 90B/27
-records containing, 63/146, see 90B/105
notice of, 63/133
-minimum periods, 63/133
-persons to be given, 63/134
powers of court to convene, 63/135
shareholders, of compensation for loss of office, in connection with, 63/188(4 & 5)
voting at, 63/137 [see **Votes**]

MEMBERS

[see **Subscribers**]
alteration of status of in winding up, by the court, void, 63/218
-voluntary, void, 63/255
arrangements, scheme of, with, 63/201-AM 82/I & 202-AM 82/I, see 83/30(14a) & 38(10) & 1987/137
articles of association, and, 63/25
balance sheet, entitled to copies of, 63/159-AM 82/I
becoming a member, 63/31
body corporate cannot be, of its holding company, 63/32, see 90B/224
death in case of, contributory who is, 63/210
deceased, transfer of shares by personal representatives of, 63/82
documents, may apply to court to enforce company's duty to deliver, 63/371
existing, issue of prospectus to, 63/44(7)
general meeting, notice of, right to, 63/134, see 83/38(6)
holding company, of, 63/32, see 90B/224
increase of, company limited by guarantee or unlimited company, notice to registrar, 63/12-AM 82/I
index of, 63/117 & 378
liability for debts, where business carried on without minimum number, 63/36
liability to contribute to share capital, increase not binding without consent, 63/27
meaning of, 63/31
meeting, may be called by, where no provision in articles, 63/134
-requisitioning of, by, 63/132
memorandum and articles, effect on, 63/25
memorandum, entitled to require copy of, 63/29
minimum number, 63/5
oppressed, relief by court, 63/205, see 90/5(4)
prosecution of, on winding up, 63/299-AM 90B/143, see 90B/179
reduction of, below legal minimum, 63/36

continued

Members continued
-ground for winding up, 63/213
reduction of capital, liability of, after, 63/76
register of, [see **Register of Members**]
register of members, 63/116-AM 82/20-AM 82/I
-form of, 63/378
-open to inspection, 63/119-AM 82/I, see 90B/105 & 244
-particulars in, 63/116-AM 82/20
-rectification of, 63/122
.application for, 63/122
-registered office, kept at, 63/116
register of, prima facie evidence of contents, 63/124
relief, alternative to winding up, may petition for, 63/205-AM 82/I, see 83/38(10) & 41(4c) & 90/5(6)
requisition of extraordinary general meeting by, 63/132
share warrant, bearer of, may be deemed to be, 63/118
trust and, 63/123
voluntary winding up, [see **Winding up, Voluntary**]
winding up, liability of, and of past, on, 63/207
winding up, petition for, 63/213

MEMORANDUM OF ASSOCIATION

Act, application by provisions of, overriding, 63/2(4)
alteration of
-by court in relief of minority, effect of, 63/205(4), see 90/5(4)
-capital conditions in, 63/68
.by reduction of capital, 63/72-AM 90B/231(1), 63/75, see 83/17(1) & 38(3c) & 43(3) & 90B/239 & 260(1) & 1989/78
.directors' liability, unlimited, by making, 63/198
.liability of members not to be increased by, 63/27
-clauses other than obligatory clauses, 63/28
-objects in, how effected, 63/10
.by company entitled to dispense with "limited" as part of its name, 63/24(7)
-pre-emption rights, and, 83/23, see 90B/260(2) & 1989/78
-provisions not necessarily contained in, 63/28-AM 83/I

continued

Memorandum of association continued
-requirements to be observed, 63/30
-restrictions on, 63/9
-to be embodied in copies, 63/30-AM 82/I
association clause and subscription to, 63/5
appropriate form, 63/6-AM 83/I, see 1989/78 & 90B/253
borrowing powers, and, 63/115-AM 82/I-AM 83/I
capital clause
-constructive notice of, [see **Ultra Vires rule**]
-effect of, 63/25 & 27
-essential features of, 63/6, see 1989/78
compromise or arrangement, order sanctioning to be annexed to, 63/201(5), see 1987/137
copy of, issued after alteration, to contain alterations, 63/30
-members entitled to, 63/29
extent to which company and members bound by, 63/25
form of, 63/16 & 395-AM 83/I & 396
guarantee, company limited by, 63/26
liability of directors, may be unlimited, 63/197-AM 82/I & 198
liability of members, limited, to be stated in memorandum, 63/6, see 1989/78
matters required to be stated in, 63/6-AM 83/I, see 1989/78 & 90B/253
meaning of, 63/2(1)
name clause, 63/6-AM 83/I, see 1989/78
objects clause
-alteration of, special resolution by, 63/10
.dissenting minority, and, 63/10-AM 83/I
-alteration of, special resolution by, registration of, 63/10-AM 83/I
-ultra vires rule, 63/8, 1973/163/6
procedure of variation of shareholders' rights, and, 63/78-AM 82/I, see 83/38(8)
public document, 63/370
public limited company, of, 83/II
registration of, 63/17, see 82/3 & 5
-effect of, 63/18

continued

Memorandum of association continued
requirements with respect to, 63/6-AM 83/I, see 1989/78
share capital, amount to be stated in, 63/6(4), see 1989/78
stamp on, 63/7
statutory form, 63/16 [see **Tables B, C, D, E**]
subscribers to, to pay cash for shares (public limited company), 83/35
subscribers to, to sign articles, 63/11-AM 82/2
-members, deemed to have agreed, to become, 63/31
-shares, to write number of, to be taken by, 63/6, see 1989/78
-signature of, to be attested, 63/7
subscription of, 63/5
subscription of, necessary for incorporation of company, 63/5

MEMORANDUM OF SATISFACTION

whole or partial, entry of, on register of charges, 63/105

MERGERS

[see **Reconstruction**]
application of principal Act to, Mergers, Takeovers & Monopolies (Control) Act, 1978
automatic deferral of, for three months, 78/3 & 6
compensation for loss of office on, 63/187 & 188
conditions, subject to, 78/11
control of, 78
decision by Minister to refer to Examiner, 78/7
enterprises, ceasing to be distinct, 78/1(3)
investigation, merger situation, qualifying for, 78/2
notification in writing to Minister, 78/5
reference in anticipation of, 78/7
report by Examiner to Minister, 78/8
Restrictive Practices Commission, reference to, 78/10
Restrictive Practices, Examiner of, function of in relation to, 78/8
safeguards for shareholders and creditors, 63/204, see 1987/137

MINIMUM SUBSCRIPTION

authorised minimum distinguished, 83/22
meaning of, 63/53-AM 83/I, see 83/22(2 & 36)
provisions as to, 63/53

MINISTER

accounts, class of company may be exempted from certain requirements as to, by, 63/VIpIII
-may alter provisions as to, by order, 63/395-AM 83/I, 86/24
-to enable subsidiary's and holding company's year to coincide, 63/153(2)
alteration of Tables A-E by statutory instrument, 63/395(2)-AM 83/I
annual report of, 63/392
annual return, may by order alter form of, 63/395(2)-AM 83/I
apply to judge for inspection and production of books may, 63/384
auditors, consultation regarding standards and qualifications, by, 90B/190
auditors, powers of, where none appointed, 63/160(4)
companies allowed by, to dispense with the word "limited" or "teoranta", 63/24
-notice of resolution altering objects, to be given to, 63/10(8)
documents of, how authenticated, 63/394
documents, power to require production, 90B/19
expenses incurred in the administration of Act, by, 63/393
fees, may alter by order, 63/395-AM 83/I
general meeting, may direct calling of, when, 63/131(3)
inspector, power to apply for appointment of, 90B/8
inspector's report, power to present petition for winding up following receipt of, 90B/12(2)
investigation of affairs of company
-application for, to, 90B/8 (replacing 63/165)

continued

Minister continued
-expenses of, to be paid in first instance by, 90B/13 (replacing 63/171)
investigation of bodies incorporated outside State, 90B/17
meetings in connection with compensation for loss of office to directors, application as to, to, 63/188(4)
misfeasance, fraud or misconduct, may bring proceedings for, (63/170(4 & 5) repealed by 90B/6)
name of company, powers of, as to change of, 63/23
-discretion as to, of, 63/21
-not formed under Act registering thereunder powers of as to, 63/334
orders under 90B, power to revoke or amend, 90B/5
ownership of company, investigation of, 90B/14
registration of companies, general powers of, in connection with, 63/368
regulations, powers to make in connection with
-acquisition of own shares and shares in holding company, 90B/228
-auditors, to make supplementary regulations relating to approval of qualifications, 90B/201
-minimum allotted share capital in company where person under disqualification order is to be director, variation of, 90B/158
-insider dealings, supplementary regulations, 90B/121
-investigations, supplementary regulations, 90B/24
-investment companies (UCITS), supplementary regulations, 90B/261
-liquidator's qualifications, 90B/237
-receiver's qualifications, 90B/237
relief, power to petition court for, where company's conduct "oppressive" to member(s), 63/205(2), see 90/5(4)
shares and debentures
-interests in, power to investigate, 90B/15
-power to impose restrictions on, 90B/16
summary proceedings by, 90B/240 (63/385-AM 82/I-AM 86/22(4) repealed by 90B/6)

continued

Minister continued
unregistered companies, powers of, in connection with
application of Act to, 63/377(2), see 90B/19 & 250 & S
winding up
-petition, power to present, 90B/12(2)
-relief alternative to, may petition for, when, 63/205(2), see 90/5(4)

MINORITY RIGHTS

[see **Dissenting members**]
alteration of objects, right to apply to court, 63/10-AM 83/I, see 83/38(10) & 41(3c)
"alternative remedy", 63/205, see 90/5(4) [see **Alternative remedy**]
application for investigation of company's affairs, [see **Investigations**]
application to court to remedy state of affairs complained of, 63/205, see 90/5(4)
minorities, oppression of, 63/205, see 90/5(4)
oppression, and, 63/205, see 90/5(4)
power of company to acquire shares of, when scheme approved by majority, 63/204, see 1987/137
proceedings by Minister, [see **Minister**]
public limited company re-registering as private, right to apply to court, 83/15
requisition of extraordinary general meeting, 63/132
variation of rights attached to shares, right to apply to court, 63/78-AM 82/I, see 83/38(8)

MINUTE BOOK

how to be kept, 63/378

MINUTES

director's duty to keep, 63/378-AM 82/I
form of, 63/378
general meetings of, inspection and copies of books containing, 63/146, see 90B/105

continued

Minutes continued
inspection of, by members, 63/146, see 90B/105
meetings, of, 63/145-AM 82/I, 63/146, see 90B/27(3)
meetings of directors, of, 63/145, see 90B/27(3)
proceedings of, to be kept and when evidence, 63/145, see 90B/27(3)

MISFEASANCE

Minister may take proceedings for, when, (63/170(4) repealed by 90B/6)
promoter or officer of, proceedings for, 90B/142 (replacing 63/298), see 90B/251, 63/310

MISLEADING NAME

[see **Name of company**]

MODIFIED ACCOUNTS

power of small or medium-sized company to file, [see **Accounts**]

MONEYLENDER

[see **Bankers; Loans etc. to directors and connected persons**]
financial assistance for acquisition of shares, 63/60(13), see 90B/155 & 224 & 260(1) & 1989/78

MORTGAGE

debenture, and, 63/94
included in expression "charge", 63/99(10)

NAME OF COMPANY

[see **Business names**]

continued

Name of company continued
"and reduced", when added to, 63/74(2)
approval, names requiring, 63/21
bill of exchange, and, 63/114-AM 82/I
business letters, on, 63/114-AM 82/I
"Chamber of Commerce", when, must be altered by deletion of words, 63/24(8)
change of, 63/23
-by omission of "limited", 63/24(2)
change of, on re-registration of company as public limited company, 83/9
cheque, and, 63/114-AM 82/I
classification of company, inclusion of indication of, 63/6-AM 83/I, see 1989/78
common seal, on, 63/114-AM 82/I
companies registered under 63/pIX, 63/334 & 335-AM 83/I
compulsory change of, 63/23(2)
"cuideachta phoibli theoranta", 83/4
display of, 63/114
foreign company, 63/355
liability of director and officer of company, and, 63/114-AM 82/I
limited liability must be brought to notice of public, 63/114-AM 82/I
"limited", licence to dispense with use of, as part of, 63/24
"limited", penalty for improper use, 63/381
"limited", to be part of, 63/335-AM 83/I, 83/58
"limited", unincorporated persons may not use as part of name, 63/381
memorandum of association, to be stated in, 63/6-AM 83/I, see 1989/78
Minister's discretion as to, 63/21
misleading, trading under, an offence, 83/56
not registered under Act, registering under, 63/334
offences in relation to, 83/56
office premises, on, 63/114-AM 82/I
part of, must be when, 63/6-AM 83/I, see 1989/78
"public limited company", 83/4

continued

Name of company continued
refusal of registration of, 63/21
-appeal against, 63/21
undesirable, 63/21
where, must be written or displayed, 63/114-AM 83/I
words to be included in, 63/6-AM 83/I, see 1989/78

NEGLIGENT MIS-STATEMENT

prospectus, in, action for damages for, 63/49

NON-CASH ASSETS

acquisition of, by public limited company from subscribers etc., 83/32
meaning, 83/2(1)

NOTES TO THE ACCOUNTS

[see **Accounts; Balance sheet; Profit and loss account**]
accounting policies, disclosure of, 86/S24
annexed document, or, 86/S23(2)
balance sheet, to, general, 86/S25-37
classes of business, 86/S41 [see **Directors' report**]
comparative figures, 86/S44
depreciation and diminution in value of assets, policy as to, 86/S24
directors' emoluments, 63/191(6), see 86/S49
directors' interest in company's shares, 90B/41(3)
dividend, 86/4(15), S25 & 35 & 37
employees, 86/S38 & 42 & 74
fixed assets, 86/S25 & 29 & 30 & 60
foreign currencies, Irish currency equivalents, 86/S44
guarantees and other financial commitments, 86/S25 & 36
income and expenditure, 86/S38 & 39 & 43
indebtedness, 86/S34 & 35
information which may be given as, 86/4(7)
investments, 86/S25 & 31 & 39 & 66

continued

Notes to accounts continued
loans, 86/S25 & 37 & 67
preceding year adjustments, 86/S43
profit and loss account, to, general, 86/S38-43
purchase price or production cost of asset, unknown, 86/S25 & 37 & 71
reserves and provisions, 86/S25 & 32 & 69 & 70
share capital and debentures, 86/S25-28
taxation, 86/S25 & 33 & 38 & 40
transactions which are exceptional, 86/S38 & 43
turnover, 86/S38 & 41 & 75 [see **Directors' report**]

NOTICE

defunct company, of striking off register, 63/311(5), see 83/8(2)
directors, general, by, of interest in contracts, 63/194(3), see 90B/27(3) & 47
-and secretary, duty of, to give to company of certain matters, 63/193-AM 82/I-AM 90B/53(11)
dissenting shareholder, for acquisition of shares of, 63/204, see 1987/137
meeting, annual general, of, 63/131
meeting, of
-auditor to be given, 90B/193(5) (63/163 repealed by 90B/6)
-compromise or arrangement, in connection with, 63/202, see 1987/137 & 90/23(7)
-length of, 63/133
-service of, where no provisions as to, in articles, 63/134
-proxies, statement as to, to be contained in, 63/136(3)-AM 82/I
special resolution, of, 63/141
voluntary winding up, of appointment of liquidator in, 63/278
-creditors, of, final meeting in, 63/273(2)
-of meeting of creditors for, 63/266(2)-AM 90B/130, see 90B/131
-members, of final meeting, in, 63/263(2)
-that resolution for, passed, 63/252-AM 82/I

NUMBERING

of shares, when not required, 63/80(2)

OBJECTS

company of, to be stated in memorandum, 63/6-AM 83/I, see 1989/78
how altered, 63/10(1 & 2)

OFFENCE

antecedent to or in course of winding up, by officer of company, 63/293-AM 82/I
-by other persons, 63/293(3)
destruction or falsification of books or papers is, 90B/243 (63/294-AM 82/I repealed by 90B/6)
foreign company, in connection with, penalty for, 63/358-AM 82/I
liabilities of officers and members, 90B/241
prosecution of, by summary proceedings, time for, 90B/240 (63/385-AM 82/I-AM 86/22(4) repealed by 90B/6)
provisions as to, 90B/240
winding up, disclosed in, inquiry into and prosecution of, 63/299-AM 90B/143, see 90B/179

OFFER OF SHARES OR DEBENTURES TO PUBLIC

[see **Allotment of shares; Prospectus**]
allotment of shares or debentures with a view to, meaning of, 63/51(2), see 83/21(2)
allotment of shares or debentures with a view to, private company, prohibited, 63/33, see 83/14(2b)
allotment of shares or debentures with a view to, subsequent written offer by allottee deemed a prospectus, 63/51, see 83/21(2)
foreign company, by, 63/361-367

continued

Offer of shares or debentures to public continued
meaning of, 63/61-AM 90B/238, see 83/21(2)
private company, prohibited, 83/21
prospectus required, 63/44

OFFICER

[see **Directors**]
auditor, disqualified from being, 90B/187 (63/162-AM 82/6 repealed by 90B/6), see 82/13 & 83/18(46)
books of account, of company, liability of, for not keeping proper, 90B/203 (63/296-AM 82/I repealed by 90B/6)
defrauding of creditors prior to winding up, offence, 63/295-AM 82/I, see 90B/251
disqualification from acting as, 90B/160 [see **Disqualification order**]
duty of, to disclose certain matters to company, 63/193(3)-AM 90B/53(11)
examination of, in winding up by the court, 90B/126 (replacing 63/245), see 90B/251
false information to auditor, penalties for, 90B/197
falsification of books by, 90B/243
fraud of, where company subsequently wound up, 63/295-AM 82/I, see 90B/251
fraud, misapplication of funds etc., power of court to investigate and order repayment, 90B/139 (90/35 deleted 90B/180)
fraud, misapplication of funds etc., power of court to investigate and order repayment, 90B/139
fraudulent trading, criminal and civil liability, 90B/137-138 (90/34 & 33 deleted 90B/180)
indemnity out of assets, in defending certain proceedings, 63/200-AM 83/I
investigation, duties of, in, 90B/10 (replacing 63/168-AM 82/7)
liability of, avoidance provisions void, 63/200-AM 83/I
loans etc. to, disclosure in notes to accounts, 90B/41(3)
meaning of, 63/2(1)
meeting of creditors, attendance at, 63/246

continued

Officer continued
misfeasance proceeding against, in winding up, 90B/142 (replacing 63/298), see 90B/251
name of company, not using, when personally liable, 63/114(4)-AM 82/I
offences by, antecedent to or in course of winding up, 63/293
officer "in default", 63/383
reduction of capital, offences by, in connection with, 63/77-AM 82/I
relief, power of court to grant in proceedings for negligence etc., 63/391

"OLD PUBLIC LIMITED COMPANY"

failure to obtain new classification, 83/13 & 16
meaning, 83/12
re-registration of, 83/12

OPERATIVE DATES
Companies Act, 1963 1 April 1964
Companies (Amendment) Act, 1977 1 April 1978
Companies (Amendment) Act, 1982 3 August 1982
Companies (Amendment) Act, 1983 13 October 1983
Companies (Amendment) Act, 1986 1 August 1986 (except s 7(1) (a)(ii) & s 8(7) & (8))
Companies (Amendment) Act, 1990 29 August 1990
Companies Act, 1990 27 December 1990 (only in respect of ss 1-5, 107-121, 180 (other than subsections 1g, 2 & 3), 181, 235, 238-240, 242, 244, 245, 247)
1 February 1991 (only in respect of ss 15,16, 19-21, 23-27, 29-49, 52, 243, 252-262)

OPTIONS

[see **Directors' interests in shares etc.**]

ORDER FOR GOODS

by company, in liquidation, to state fact, 63/303-AM 82/I
-when receiver or manager appointed, to state fact, 63/317-AM 82/I

ORDER FORMS

details to be disclosed on, 1973/163/9

OWNERSHIP OF COMPANY

investigation of, [see **Disclosure of interests in shares of public limited company; Investigations; Investigation by public limited company of interests in its shares**]

PARTNERSHIP

banking, prohibition on having more than ten members, 63/372
limited, may be wound up under Act, (63/345(8) repealed by Second Schedule, Bankruptcy Act, 1988)
of more than twenty persons, illegal, 63/376
-exemption for accountants and solicitors, 82/13
-exemption for thoroughbred horse breeders, 1988/54
-Minister may permit other exemptions, 82/13

PATENT

or licence under, charge on, requires registration, 63/99(2)

PENSIONS, DIRECTORS OF

not included in compensation for loss of office, when, 63/189(3)
particulars of, to be given in accounts, 63/191

PENSION SCHEME

residual interests under, 83/42 & 43

PERSONATION

of holder of share warrant, 63/90-AM 82/I

PERPETUAL DEBENTURES, 63/94

PERSONAL REPRESENTATIVE

liability, on death of contributory, 63/210
registration as member of company, 63/82 & 87-AM 77/5(1)
title to shares, on death of member, 63/87(2)
transmission of shares to, 63/81
transfer of shares by, 63/82

PETITION

[see **Winding up, court, by**]
relief alternative to winding up, for, 63/205-AM 82/I, see 83/38(10) & 41(4c) & 90/5(4)
winding up, for, 63/215

"p.l.c."

public limited company may use abbreviation when name in English, 83/4

POLL

[see **General meeting**]
procedure, at general meeting, 63/137
right to demand on special resolution, 63/141(3)
votes on, member need not use all in same way, 63/138
voting on, manner of, 63/138

PRE-EMPTION, RIGHT OF

allotment of shares, in, 83/20
alteration of memorandum or articles, and, 83/23, see 90B/260(2) & 1989/78
duty of company not to allot "equity securities" without first offering them to existing shareholders, 83/23, see 90B/260(2) & 1989/78
exclusion of application of, 83/23, see 90B/260(2) & 1989/78
extent of, 83/23, see 90B/260(2) & 1989/78
meaning of, 83/23, see 90B/260(2) & 1989/78
preference shares, and, 83/23, see 90B/260(2) & 1989/78

PREFERENCE SHARES

[see **Redeemable preference shares; Redemption of shares; Share capital; Shares**]
redeemable, power to issue, (63/64-AM 83/I cesser 90B/220)

PREFERENTIAL PAYMENTS

floating charge, on enforcement of, 63/98
floating charge, where possession taken of property subject to, 63/98
winding up, in, 63/285-AM 82/10-AM 90B/134
-distress within three months of, a first charge on, 63/285(9)

PRE-INCORPORATION CONTRACTS

ratification of, 63/37

PRELIMINARY EXPENSES

accounts, to be shown in, 63/VIpI
assets, not to be treated as, 86/4(12)
prospectus, information, as to, to be given in, 63/IIIpIpIII
share premium account may be used to write off, 63/62(2)-AM 83/I

PREMIUM

shares issued at, provisions applicable where, 63/62-AM 90B/231(1), see 90B/207
[see **Share premium account**]

PRESCRIBED

meaning of, 63/2(1)

PRIVATE COMPANY

annual return, and, 63/125 & 129
annual return of, certificates required to be sent with, 63/129
articles of association, 63/13, Table A pII
basic form of company, as, 63/33
certificate with annual return, 63/129
commencement of business, provisions as to, do not apply to, 63/115(7)
commission for share subscription, notice to registrar, 63/59-AM 82/I
company ceasing to be, to file statement in lieu of prospectus, 63/35-AM 83/I, 63/II
conversion of public limited company into, 83/14
default by, in complying with provisions required to constitute, 63/34
director, restrictions on appointment or advertisement of do not apply to, or to company originally a, 63/179(5)
directors of, 63/174
financial assistance for purchase of own shares, power to give in certain cases, 63/60, see 90B/155 & 224 & 260(1) & 1989/78
forfeiture of privileges and exemptions, 63/34
formation of, 63/5
holding company, as, group accounts, and, 63/154-AM 82/I, see 86/S45(1)
meaning of, 63/33
members, effect of having less than two, 63/36

continued

Private company continued
memorandum of association, statutory form, 63/6-AM 83/I, see 1989/78
minimum number of two members, 63/5(1)
name, [see **Name of company**]
offer of shares or debentures to public prohibited, 83/21
provisions as to articles of, prohibiting invitation to public, construction of, 63/61-AM 90B/238, see 83/21(2)
re-registration as public limited company, 83/9 & 10
re-registration of "old public limited company" as, 83/13
shares, prohibition on offer to public, 83/21
statement in lieu of prospectus not required in case of, 63/54(3)-AM 83/I

PROBATE

evidence of grant of, 63/87(2)

PROCEEDINGS

Minister by, in name of body corporate, when may be taken, (63/170(4) repealed by 90B/6)
company not formed under Act, continued against, after registration, 63/339
privileged communication to solicitor not required to be disclosed in, 63/387
former Companies Acts, taken under, not affected by Act, 63/3(2)
limited company by, court may order security for costs to be given in, 63/390
liquidator may bring or defend, in official name, when, 63/230
-in name of company, when, 63/231-AM 90B/124
relief, court may grant in, for negligence, default, breach of duty or breach of trust, 63/391
summary, for offences, provisions as to, 90B/240 (63/385 repealed by 90B/6)

continued

Proceedings continued
winding up, court may stay, 63/234
winding up order, stay of, on, 63/222
-in case of companies not formed but registered under Act, 63/343
-in case of unregistered companies, 63/348
winding up petition, stay or restraint of, after presentation of, 63/217

PROFIT AND LOSS ACCOUNT

[see **Accounts**]
additional disclosures in, 86/4(5)
balance sheet, to be annexed to, 63/157-AM 82/I
classes of business, 86/S38 & 41
comparative figures to be shown in, 86/4(8)
consolidated, [see **Group Accounts**]
directors' duty to prepare, 63/148-AM 82/I, see 83/49 & 86/3 & 90B/43
employees, particulars of, 86/S38 & 42 & 74
exemptions from, 63/VI
form and contents of, 63/149-AM 82/I, 63/VI, 86/3-5 & S, see 83/9(12,13a) & 49 & III
-when company has a subsidiary, 63/149(4), 86/16 & 17
general meeting, to be laid before company in, in every year, 63/148(2), see 90B/43, 86/3
general rules as to, 86/3 & S1-3
group, [see **Group Accounts**]
holding company, of, [see **Group Accounts**]
income and expenditure, 86/S38 & 39 & 43
members, right to receive copies, 63/159-AM 82/I
non-profit company, of, 63/149(8)
notes to, 86/S38-43
preceding year adjustments, 86/S43
references to, includes certain notes on, and other documents, 63/149(8)
signing of, 63/156
subsidiary, of, [see **Group Accounts**]
tax, 86/S38 & 40
transactions which are exceptional, 86/S38 & 43
turnover, 86/S38 & 41 & 75

PROFITS

[see **Distributions**]
available for distribution, 86/S45
distribution of, [see **Distribution of profits**]
meaning of, 83/51(2)(d & e)-AM 90B/232, see 1989/78
realised, meaning of, 63/149, 83/45, see 90B/260(2) & 1989/78
"realised", 86/S72
unrealised, application in paying up shares, 83/45(3) & 51(6), see 90B/260(2) & 1989/78

PROMISSORY NOTE

how made, accepted and endorsed on behalf of a company, 63/39
name of company to be on, 63/114
when deemed to be made etc., by company, 63/39

PROMOTER

definition, for provisions imposing civil liability for mis-statement in a prospectus, 63/49(8)
disqualification of person from acting as, 90B/160 (63/184-AM 82/I repealed by 90B/6) [see **Disqualification order**]
meaning of, 63/49(8)
misfeasance, proceedings against, in winding up, 90B/142 (replacing 63/298), see 90B/251
pre-incorporation contracts, and, 63/37
prospectus, interest of, to be stated in, 63/IIIpl/13
-liability of, for untrue statements in, 63/49
remuneration of, 63/37

PROOF

debts and claims, admissible to, 63/283
-of, in case of insolvent company, 63/284
-of, time may be fixed for, 63/241
disclaimer, by person injured by, 63/290(9)

PROPERTY OF COMPANY

[see **Assets; Charges; Distributions; Receiver;** and appropriate headings relating to **Winding up**]

PROPERTY TRANSACTIONS

substantial, involving director or connected persons, restrictions on, 90B/29

PROSPECTUS

abridged, 63/45
accountant's report prior to issue, 63/46-AM 82/I, 63/III
adequate information in, 63/44-52, 63/III
allotment of shares or debentures after, 63/56-AM 82/I
application for shares or debentures, form of, to be accompanied by, when, 63/44(3 & 4)
auditors' report prior to issue, 63/46-AM 82/I, 63/III
contents of, requirements as to, 63/44-52, 63/III
contract referred to in, may only be varied with approval of statutory meeting, (63/48 repealed 83/III)
dated, to be, 63/43
directors' liability, 63/49, 63/50-AM 82/I
director, person may not be named in as, when, 63/179
document deemed to be, 63/51, see 83/21(2)
discount, statement as to shares issued at, to be contained in, (63/63(4) repealed 83/III), see 83/27(4)
exemptions and relaxations of restrictions on, 63/45
existing members or debenture holders, certain provisions excluded in case of issue of, to, 63/44(7)
expert, containing statement by, provision as to, 63/46-AM 82/I
foreign company of, [see **Foreign Company**]
form of application for shares must be accompanied by, 63/44(3 & 4)

continued

Prospectus continued
issue of, provisions as to registration to be complied with before, 63/47-AM 82/I
issued generally, application and allotment in pursuance of, 63/56-AM 82/I
-documents to be attached to, and statements to be endorsed on, 63/47(1)
-requirement as to, modified in certain cases, 63/45
matters to be stated and reports to be set out in, 63/44, 63/III
meaning of, 63/2(1)
mis-statement in
-civil liability for, 63/49
-criminal liability for, 63/50-AM 82/I
non-compliance with provisions as to, not involving liability, when, 63/44(5)
offer for sale, document containing, when deemed to be a, 63/51, see 83/21(2)
"offer to public", 63/61-AM 90B/238
permission to deal, containing statement as to, provisions as to, 63/57
promoters, disclosures in relation to, 63/III
reports in, 63/III
registration of, and provisions as to, 63/47-AM 82/I
restrictions on alterations of terms in, (63/48 repealed 83/III)
statement, deemed to be included in, what is, 63/52
-in lieu of, [see **Statement in Lieu of Prospectus**]
-untrue, in
.civil liability for, 63/49
.criminal liability for, 63/50-AM 82/I
-what deemed to be, 63/52
stock exchange quotation, and, 63/57-AM 82/I

PROVISIONAL LIQUIDATOR

appointment of, and powers of, 63/226
-examination of officers and others after, 90B/126 (replacing 63/245)
exception, rights of, as to goods taken in, 63/292

continued

Provisional liquidator continued
proceedings stayed on appointment of, 63/222
property of the company, to take custody of, 63/229
statement of affairs, required on appointment of, 63/224, see 90B/18

PROVISIONS

how shown in accounts, 63/VI, 86

PROXY

appointment of, 63/136-AM 82/I
confers authority to demand poll, 63/137
invitations to appoint, not to be sent to some members only, 63/136(5)-AM 82/I
provisions as to, 63/136-AM 82/I
voting at meetings, and, 63/136-AM 82/I
voting on a poll by, 63/138
winding up, at a meeting of creditors or contributories in a, Rules Or74 r75-84

PRUDENCE - ACCOUNTING PRINCIPLE

requirement, 86/5

PUBLIC

offering to, meaning of, 63/61-AM 90B/238
shares or debentures not offered to, prospectus not required to accompany form of application for, 63/44(4)

PUBLICITY

accounting records, 90B/202(6)
articles of association, copies to members, 63/29
charges, copy of instrument creating, 63/109 & 110
charges, register of, 63/103

continued

Publicity continued
company's name etc., [see **Business letters; Documents; Order forms; Registered office**]
directors and secretaries, register of, 90B/51 (replacing 63/195-AM 82/8), see 82/3(2) & 8(2)
directors' service contracts, inspection, 90B/50
general meetings, minutes, inspection, 63/146, see 90B/105
liquidator to notify of his appointment, in voluntary winding up to registrar, 63/278
memorandum of association and amendments, copy to members, 63/29 & 30
publication in "Iris Oifigiuil" by company of notification of receipt or issue of company documents etc., 1973/163/4
register of directors' interest in shares etc., 90B/59-60

PUBLIC LIMITED COMPANY

articles of association, statutory form, 63/I (Table A pl)
certificate to commence business, 83/6, see 90B/256(2) & 1989/78
charges on own shares, 83/44
directors of, 63/174
interests in shares in, disclosure of, and investigation of [see **Disclosure of interests in shares of public limited company; Investigation by a public limited company of interests in its shares**]
joint stock company, application to register as, 83/18
meaning of, 83/2(1)
memorandum of association, statutory form, 83/II
minimum number of seven members, 63/5
minimum subscription for shares of, 63/53
name of, [see **Name of company**]
"old", [see **"Old public limited company"**]
name of public limited company in English must end with, 83/4
private company, conversion into, 83/14 & 15
continued

Public limited company continued
reduction of allotted share capital below authorised minimum, 83/40, see 90B/260(2) & 1989/78
registration (or re-registration) as, conditions relating to share capital, 83/10
re-registration of private company as, 83/9 & 10
-application for, 83/9
-special resolution, 83/9
-steps which must be taken, 83/9
restrictions on commencement of business, 83/6, see 90B/256 & 1989/78
restrictions on distributions of profits, and, 83/45-51, see 90B/260(2) & 1989/78
secretary, qualifications of, 90B/236
share capital, requirements to be met, 83/10 & 19
treatment of shares held by or on behalf of, 83/43-AM 90B/232

PURCHASE BY COMPANY OF ITS OWN SHARES

company may not give financial assistance for, of its or its holding company's shares, 63/60, see 90B/155 & 224 & 260(1) & 1989/78
[see **Acquisition by Company of its own Shares; Financial Assistance by Company for Acquisition of its own shares**]

QUALIFICATION

shares, duty to obtain and effect of ceasing to hold, 63/180, see 90B/110
-undertaking to take, effect of, 63/179(2)

QUASI-LOAN

[see **Loans etc. to directors and connected persons**]
breach of prohibitions, civil remedies, 90B/38
breach of prohibitions, criminal penalties, 90B/40
continued

Quasi-loan continued
disclosure by company, 90B/41-43
meaning, 90B/25(1)
prohibition on, to directors and connected persons, 90B/31

QUORUM

general provisions as to, when no provision in articles, 63/134

REALISED LOSS

distribution of profits, and, 83/45, see 90B/260(2) & 1989/78

RECEIVER

accounts and information to be furnished by, 63/319-AM 82/I, see 90B/145
accounts of, to be delivered to registrar, 63/321-AM 82/I-AM 90B/145
application for direction, 90B/171 (replacing 63/316(1))
appointed out of court
-accounts, duty of, as to, 63/321-AM 82/I-AM 90B/145
-floating charge, to enforce, 63/319(3), 63/320(4)
-liability of, on contracts, 63/316(2)
-may apply to court for directions, 90B/171 (replacing 63/316(1))
-notification of, 63/107-AM 82/I
-remuneration of, may be fixed by court on application of liquidator, 63/318, 1964/45/3
appointment of, and ceasing to act of, notice to registrar, 63/107-AM 82/I
-fact of, to be stated on business letters, etc., 63/317
appointment of new, 90B/175
assets improperly transferred, court may order return, 90B/178

continued

Receiver continued
bankrupt, undischarged, may not be, 90B/170 (replacing 63/315-AM 82/I), see 90B/237
body corporate may not be, 63/314
court may order restricted powers or removal, on appointment of liquidator, 90B/176
-receiver may appear and be heard, 90B/176
disqualification for appointment as, 90B/170
duty to notify company, 63/319-AM 82/I, see 90B/145
liability on contracts, 63/316(2)
liquidator, when same person as, 63/319(5)
meaning of, 63/319 & 323
non-cash asset, restriction on sale to officer or former officer of company, 90B/172(3)
offence disclosed in, duties of, as to, 90B/179, see 63/299(2)-AM 90B/143
officer, may apply to court to make personally liable, 90B/138
preferential payments by, 63/98
property sale, duty to get best price reasonably available, 90B/172
qualification of, Minister's powers to amend by regulations, 90B/237
relieved of liability where charge defective, 63/316(3)
removal of, 90B/175
remuneration of, 63/318(1)
resignation of, 90B/177
returns, enforcement of duty to make, 63/322
returns, penalty for default in making, 90B/145
scope of provisions applying to, 63/323
statement of affairs, to be submitted to, 63/319(1)
statement of company's affairs by directors etc., where appointed in respect of floating charge, 63/320
statement of company's affairs prepared by directors etc. to be notified to registrar, 63/320 & 321
statement of affairs under 63/319-320, court to make order if not submitted, 90B/174
-duty to report whether any officer director or member is subject to a declaration of personal liability for all or any part of debts of company or is subject to
continued

Receiver continued
or deemed to be subject to a disqualification order, 90B/144
who may apply to court for directions, 90B/171

RECONSTRUCTION

compromise or arrangement involving, 63/203, see 1987/137
powers of court to facilitate, on a compromise or arrangement with creditors or members, 63/201-AM 82/I, see 83/30(14a) & 38(10), 63/203-AM 82/I, see 83/38(10) & 1987/137
voluntary winding up, by, 63/260, see 83/30(14a) & 1987/137
-dissentient shareholders, and, 63/260, see 1987/137
-members' winding up, and, 63/260, see 1987/137
-no application to court necessary, 63/260, see 1987/137
-notice by dissentient shareholder, and, 63/260(3), see 1987/137
-special resolution, and, 63/260, see 1987/137

REDEEMABLE PREFERENCE SHARES

power to issue, (63/64-AM 83/I cesser 90B/220)
provisions as to, (63/64-AM 83/I cesser 90B/220)
reduction of capital, and, (63/64(3) cesser 90B/220)
share premium account may be applied in paying premium on reduction of, 63/62(2)-AM 83/I-AM 90B/231

REDEMPTION OF SHARES

capital redemption reserve, requirement for transfer of amounts to, (63/64(1) cesser 90B/220)
conditions to be met, (63/64-AM 83/I cesser 90B/220)
new issue of shares, for purposes of redemption, (63/64(1) cesser 90B/220)
payment on redemption, out of distributable profits or new share issue, (63/64(1) cesser 90B/220)

continued

Redemption of shares continued
premium payable on redemption, (63/64-AM 83/I cesser 90B/220)
terms of redemption, may be provided in articles, (63/64(1) cesser 90B/220)

REDUCTION OF CAPITAL

authorised by articles, Rules Or75 r3
cancellation of shares, not deemed to be, 63/68(2)
confirmation of court, 63/72(2), see 1989/78 & 90B/260(1)
court, application to, to confirm, 63/73, see 83/43(3)
-order by, on application to confirm, 63/75, see 83/17(3)
how made, 63/72-AM 90B/231(1), see 83/17(1) & 38(3c) & 43(3) & 55(1c) & 90B/260(1) & 1989/78
loss of significant part of capital, where, 63/72-AM 90B/231(1), see 90B/260(1) & 1989/78
members, liability of, after, 63/76
minute of, to be confirmed by court, 63/75, see 83/17(3)
offences by officers of company in connection with, 63/77-AM 82/I
over-capitalisation, and, 63/72-AM 90B/231(1), see 90B/260(1) & 1989/78
petition to court, Rules Or75 r3
procedure for, Rules Or75 r3
protection of rights of creditors, 63/73
publication of advertisements, and, 63/73
public limited company, restrictions on, 83/17
redeeming preference shares is not, (63/64(3) cesser 90B/220)
share premium account, provisions as to, apply to, 63/62-AM 90B/231(1), see 90B/207

REGISTER OF CHARGES

registrar, kept by, 63/103
registrar, kept by, inspection of, 63/103(2)
-memorandum of satisfaction, whole or partial to be entered on, 63/105

REGISTER OF DIRECTORS AND SECRETARIES

company's duty to keep, 90B/51 (replacing 63/195)
provisions as to keeping, 90B/51 (replacing 63/195)

REGISTER OF INTERESTS IN SHARES

[see **Disclosure of interests in shares of public limited company; Investigation by a public limited company of interests in its shares**]
directors' interests, of, 90B/80 [see **Directors' interests in shares etc.**]
index of names entered on, also to be kept, 90B/80(7)
information received as a result of company's investigation into share interests, to be entered in, 90B/82
inspection and copies of, 90B/80(9)
interests in shares, notified to company, to be entered in, 90B/80(1)
obligation of public limited company to maintain, 90B/80(1)
"relevant share capital", 90B/67(2)
removal of certain entries permitted, 90B/86
removal of entries, general prohibition, 90B/87

REGISTER OF MEMBERS

agent, kept by, consequences of default, 63/120
classes of shares or of members to be shown in, 63/116
close, when company may, 63/121
company to keep, 63/116-AM 82/20-AM 82/I
evidence as to what matters, is, 63/124
index, provisions as to, when not in form of, 63/117
inspection of, and copies of, 63/119, see 90B/105 & 260
particulars to be entered in, 63/116
place, where, to be kept, 63/116(5)
-kept, other than registered office, default as to provisions where, 63/120
rectification of, 63/122

continued

Register of members continued
-in winding up, court, by, 63/235
State, must be kept at a place in, 63/116(6)
transferor may apply for transferee to be entered on, 63/83
trust, notice of, not to be entered on, 63/123

REGISTER OF SHARES OR DEBENTURES IN WHICH DIRECTORS INTERESTED

provisions as to, 90B/53-57 & 59 (replacing 63/190-AM 82/I)

REGISTERED LAND

charge on, registration, and, 63/99
floating charge, and, registration, and, 63/99

REGISTERED NUMBER

business letters and order forms, to be on, 1973/163/9

REGISTERED OFFICE

address on business letters and order forms, 63/114-AM 82/I-AM 83/I
alteration of situation of, 63/113-AM 82/4
change in situation of, to be notified to registrar within fourteen days, 82/4
documents to be kept at
-accounts, books of, 90B/202 (63/147 repealed by 90B/6)
-charges, copies of instruments creating, 63/109
-debenture holders, register of, 63/91
-directors and secretaries, register of, 90B/51 (replacing 63/195)
-directors and secretaries, register of shareholdings, 90B/53-57 & 59 (replacing 63/190)
-general meetings, minute books of, 63/146, see 90B/105
-members' register of, 63/116

continued

Registered office continued
Ireland, in, 63/113-AM 82/4
name of company on outside, 63/114
notice of situation, 63/113-AM 82/4
provisions as to, 63/113-AM 82/4, see 82/3(2c)
register of
-directors and secretaries to be kept at, 90B/51 (replacing 63/195)
-of directors' holdings of shares etc., to be kept at, 90B/53-57 & 59 (replacing 63/190)
situation of, registration of, 82/3
statement of first directors and secretary, to specify intended situation of, 82/4(2c)

REGISTERS TO BE KEPT BY COMPANY

charges, of, 63/109
debenture holders, of, 63/91-AM 82/l
directors' interests in shares etc., of, 90B/59
directors and secretaries, of, 90B/51 (replacing 63/195-AM 82/8), see 82/8(2)
directors and secretaries, of, past directorships held within past ten years to be included, 90B/51
form of, general provisions as to, 63/378-AM 77/4
how to be kept, 63/378-AM 77/4
interests in shares, of, [see **Register of interests in shares**]
members, of, [see **Register of members**]

REGISTRAR OF COMPANIES

[see **Accounts; Annual return; Charges; Foreign company ; Register of charges; Registration of companies; Registration of companies not formed under the Act;** and appropriate headings relating to **Receiver** and **Winding up**]
accounts, delivery to, [see **Accounts**]
appointment of, etc., 63/368
certificate of registration of charge, 63/104

continued

-company entitled to commence business, that, 63/115(3)
-incorporation of, (63/19-AM 82/18 repealed 83/III)
charges, register of, to be kept by, 63/103
classification system may be applied by, 90B/247
commission for share subscription where offer not made to public, notice of, 63/59-AM 82/I
companies not formed but registered under Act, duties of, as to, [see **Companies not formed under Act**]
default, may apply to court, where company in as to returns, 63/371
-where receiver in, as to returns, 63/322(2)
defunct company, may strike off register, 63/311-AM 82/11, see 82/12-AM 90B/245
documents, delivery in legible form to, 90B/248
-otherwise than in legible form, 90B/249
documents, dissolved company of, may dispose of, 63/313
-kept by, evidence of, 63/370(3)
-inspection and copies of, 63/370(1)
documents to be delivered to
-allotments, return of, 63/58-AM 82/19, see 83/31(2) & 55(1g)
-alteration of objects, on, 63/10(9)
-annual general meeting, resolution that meeting to be treated as, 63/131(5)
-annual return, 63/127
-appointment of liquidator in winding up by the court, of, 63/227-AM 82/I
-articles, 63/17, see 82/3 & 5
-charges requiring registration by, and particulars of, 63/99-AM 90B/122, 63/101
-liquidations, statements as to progress, 63/306(1)-AM 90B/145
-members, increases of, in unlimited companies and companies limited by guarantee, 63/12(3)
-memorandum, 63/17, see 82/3 & 5
-order of Court

continued

Registrar of companies continued
.declaring dissolution void, 63/310(2)-AM 82/I
.dissolution, for, 63/249(2)
.involving re-construction or amalgamation, 63/203(3)-AM 82/I, see 1987/137
.relief of minority, in, 63/205(5)-AM 82/I
.restoring company to register, 63/311(8), see 90B/246
.sanctioning compromise or arrangement, 63/201(5), see 1987/137
.staying winding up, 63/234(4)
.voluntary winding up, in, 63/280(3), see 90B/131
.winding up, for, 63/221-AM 82/I
-register of debenture holders, of place where, kept, 63/91(3)
-register of members
.rectification of, 63/122(4)
.where kept, and when location changed, 63/116(7)
duty of company to make returns etc. to, enforcement, 63/371
fees payable to, 63/369
foreign companies, by, 63/352 & 353
-ceasing to carry on business in the State, by, 63/357
-prospectus of, 63/364
meaning of, 63/2(1)
notice to be given to, appointment of liquidator in voluntary winding up, of, 63/278-AM 82/I
prospectus, 63/47(1)
prospectus, duties of in connection with registration of, 63/47-AM 82/I
publication in "Iris Oifigiuil" of notification of receipt or issue of company documents etc., 1973/163/4
receiver's abstract of receipts and payments, 63/319(2)-AM 82/I-AM 90B/145, 63/321
reduction of, capital, on, 63/75, see 83/17(3)
register of directors and secretaries, return as to, 90B/51 (replacing 63/195(6)-AM 82/8)
registered office, information as to, to be given to, 63/113-AM 82/4
resolutions, copies of what, 63/143(1)

continued

Registrar of companies continued
settlement, deed of memorandum and articles substituted of, 63/341(2)
share capital, notice of increase, cancellation, redemption, consolidation, conversion into stock, 63/69 & 70, see 90B/221 & 260(1) & 1989/78
share capital, reduction, registration of court order, 63/75
statement in lieu of prospectus, 63/35-AM 83/I
statutory report, (63/130(6) repealed 83/I)
trust, notice of, not receivable by, 63/123
voluntary winding up, creditors, return as to final meeting in, 63/273(3)-AM 82/I
-members, return as to final meeting in, 63/263(3)-AM 82/I
variation of class rights, copy of court order, 63/78-AM 82/I

REGISTRATION OF CHARGES

certificate of, 63/104
delivery of particulars by lender, 63/100-AM 82/I
extension of time period, 63/106
-creditors' rights, and, 63/106
failure, effect of, 63/99-AM 90B/122
particulars to be entered in register, 63/99-AM 90B/122
particulars to be sent to registrar within twenty-one day period, 63/99-AM 90B/122
rectification of errors, 63/106

REGISTRATION OF COMPANIES

[see **Foreign companies; Registration of companies not formed under the Act; Re-registration**]
certificate of incorporation, issue and effect, 63/18
general provisions as to, 63/368
memorandum and articles, delivery for registration, 63/17, see 82/3 & 83/5
name, [see **Name**]

continued

Registration of companies continued
not formed under Act, [see **Companies not formed under Act**]
statement of first directors and secretary, delivery with memorandum, 82/3

REGISTRATION OF COMPANIES NOT FORMED UNDER THE ACT

[see **Joint stock company**]
certificate of registration, 63/336-AM 83/I, see 83/18(6)
companies able to register, 63/328
name, requirements, 63/330-AM 83/I
procedure, 63/328 & 330-333

RELEVANT SHARES

meaning of, 83/23(13), see 90B/260(2) & 1989/78

RELIEF

of officer or auditor from liability in certain cases by the court, 63/391

RENT AND RENTCHARGE

[see **Land**]

REPEAL

of enactments and consequential provisions for continuity on, 63/3, 63/XII

REQUISITION

extraordinary general meeting, of, 63/132

RE-REGISTRATION

limited company, as unlimited, 83/52

continued

Re-registration continued
nominal value of allotted share capital falling below authorised minimum, where, 83/43
"old public limited company", provisions regulating, 83/12
private company, public limited company or "old public limited company" as, power of members to apply to cancel resolution, 83/15
private company as public limited company, 83/9 & 10
public limited company as private company, 83/14 & 15
unlimited company as limited company, 83/53
unlimited company as public limited company, 83/11

RESERVE

accounts, how dealt with in, 63/VIpl/6
capital, 63/67
-unregistered company may provide for on re-registration as limited company, 63/71

RESERVE SHARE CAPITAL

[see **Share Capital**]
limited company, power to put aside for winding up, 63/67

RESOLUTION

adjourned meeting passed at, date of, 63/144, see 90/23(6)
-of creditors and contributories, passed at, date of, 63/308
annual general meeting, that meeting be treated as, 63/131(4)
auditor, directed to preventing re-election of, extended notice to be given of, 63/161-AM 90B/184
director, for appointment of more than one, void, 63/181
-removal of, ordinary, for, 63/182
extended notice of, 63/142
generally, 63/141

continued

Resolution continued
passed at adjourned meeting of company etc., date of, 63/144, see 90/23(6)
passed at adjourned meeting of creditors or contributories, date of, 63/308
requisition, notice of, to be given on, when special, [see **Special resolution**]
voluntary winding up, for, 63/251, see 83/12(8) & 16(1c)
-copy of, to be delivered to registrar, 63/143, see 83/18(6) & 39 & 53(1) & 55(1j)
-to be advertised in "Iris Oifigiuil", 63/252-AM 82/I
winding up by the court, for, 63/213

RESTORATION OF A COMPANY

copy of court order to registrar, 63/311(8)
court's power to declare dissolution void, 63/311(8)
effect of revival on property disposed of, 63/311(8)
objection to striking off by person aggrieved, 63/311(8)
registrar's power to restore within twelve months of striking off, 90B/246

RETURNS

persistent default in making, ground for disqualification, 90B/160(2f) [see **Disqualification order**]

RETURN

allotment of share capital, to be delivered to registrar, 63/58-AM 82/19
annual, [see **Annual return**]
duty of company to make, enforcement of, 63/371
notification of changes in director etc., 90B/51 (replacing 63/195-AM 82/8), see 82/3(2)
receiver, by, 63/321-AM 82/I-AM 90B/145

RULES

general, for winding up, may be made, 63/312

SCHEME OF ARRANGEMENT

[see **Examiner**]

SEAL

common seal of company, contracts under, 63/38
name, to be engraved on, 63/114
official, for use abroad, 63/41
official seal, power to have for sealing securities etc., 77/3
power of attorney, under, effective for execution of deeds abroad, 63/41(4)
share certificate, to be under common seal or official seal, 77/3

SECRETARY

address of first, 82/3
annual return, particulars as to, to be given in, 63/125(1)
appointment of first, 82/3
assistant or deputy, 63/175(2)
change of, to be notified to registrar within fourteen days, 90B/51 (replacing 63/195(6)-AM 82/8)
company must have, 63/175(1)
director, who is also, may not act in dual capacity when, 63/177
foreign companies, details of, on registration, 63/352
foreign company of, meaning of, 63/360
indemnity of, out of assets, in defending certain proceedings, 63/200
joint, 90B/51 (replacing 63/195(4))
liability of, avoidance provisions void, 63/200
name of first, 82/3
register of, 90B/51 (replacing 63/195)
-inspection of, 90B/51 (replacing 63/195(9))
register of directors and secretaries, particulars of, to be given in, 90B/51 (replacing 63/195-AM 82/8), see 82/3

continued

Secretary continued
relief, power of court to grant in proceedings for negligence, 63/391
statement of first, on registration, 82/3
vacancy in office etc., other officer may act as, 63/175(2)

SECURITIES

Minister may make regulation for transfer of securities without written instrument, 90B/239

SECURITY

to be given by liquidator in winding up by the court, 63/228

SEQUESTRATION

void against company being wound up by the court, 63/219

SERVICE

company on, how effected, 63/379
oversea company on, how effected, 63/356

SERVICE CONTRACT

director's, company to keep available for inspection by members, 90B/50
director's, for more than five years, approval of general meeting, 90B/28
director's place kept, notice to registrar, 90B/50
shadow director's, 90B/26 & 27 & 50

SET-OFF

when allowed between company and contributory, 63/237

SHADOW DIRECTOR

provisions applying to, 90B/27

SHARE CAPITAL

[see **Allotment of shares; Capital; Shares**]
allotment, prospectus to state whether allotment will proceed if issue not fully subscribed, 83/22
authorised minimum, (public limited company), 83/2(1)
cancellation of unallotted shares, 63/68
cancellation on purchase or redemption, [see **Purchase by company of its own shares; Redemption of shares**]
issue of, [see **Allotment of shares; Shares**]
public limited company, conditions for commencement of business, 83/10
reduction of, liability of members, 63/76
reduction of, offence to conceal name of creditor, etc., 63/77
reserve share capital, 63/67 & 71
stationery, reference to be to paid-up capital, 1973/163/9

SHARE CERTIFICATE

delivery after allotment, duty of company, 63/86, see 90B/239
effect of, 63/87-AM 77/5(1)
evidence of title, as, 63/87-AM 77/5
exemption from obligations where transfer to a stock exchange nominee, 77/2
official seal for, 77/3
right of member to, 63/86, see 90B/239

SHARE DEALINGS

[see **Directors' interests in shares; Disclosure of interests in shares of public limited company; Insider dealing**]

SHARE PREMIUM ACCOUNT

premiums on issue of shares to be transferred to,
63/62-AM 90B/231(1), see 90B/207
provisions as to, 63/62-AM 90B/231(1), see 90B/207

SHAREHOLDERS

[see **Contributories; Members; Minority rights; Subscribers**]
death of, 63/81 & 82
dissenting, acquisition of shares of, 63/204, see 1987/137
duties of, 63/28
meaning of, 90B/53-57 & 59 (replacing 63/190)
meetings of, in connection with director's compensation for loss of office on transfer of shares, 63/188(4)
register of debenture holders, may inspect, 63/92, see 90B/105
variation of rights of classes of, 63/10 & 78 & 203 & 205, see 83/15 & 20 & 38 & 1987/137 & 90/5(4)
-application for, 63/78-AM 82/I
-consent of holders of three-quarters of shares, and, 63/78, 83/38, see 1987/137
-procedure contained in memorandum or articles, 63/78, 83/38, see 1987/137
-requirements for, 63/78, 83/38, see 1987/137

SHARES

[see **Share capital**]
acquisition by a company of its own, 63/32, 83/42, see 83/41-AM 90B/232(a), see 90B/224 & 227 & 260(2) & 1987/137 & 1989/78
-exceptions to general prohibition, 83/41-AM 90B/232(a), 83/42, see 90B/227 & 260(2) & 1987/137 & 1989/78
-nominee, and, 83/42
-offence in relation to, 83/57
-subsidiary, and, 63/32, see 90B/224
allotment of, [see **Allotment of shares**]

continued

Shares continued
allotment of, prohibited in certain cases unless
statement in lieu of prospectus delivered, 63/54
-return of, 63/58
allotted, payment for, 83/26
amount of, 63/6(4), see 90B/253 & 1989/78
application for, [see **Application for shares**]
applications for, and allotment of, in pursuance of
prospectus issued generally, 63/56
bonus, [see **Bonus shares**]
calls, [see **Calls**]
cancellation of, 63/68
certificates of, company's obligation in respect to,
63/86, see 90B/239
certificates, issue of, 63/86-AM 82/I, see 90B/239
class of, [see **Class**]
classes, identification in company's register of
members, 63/116
classes, variation of rights attached to, 63/78-AM 82/I,
see 83/38(8)
commission for subscription, 63/59
conditions to be met before admitted to official stock
exchange listing, 1984/282, see 1991/18
consideration other than cash, 63/58(1), 83/26
-deferred payment, 83/26
-expert's valuation and report, 83/30, see 1987/137
.contents of, 83/30, see 1987/137
-fraud, and, 83/26
-registration of contract, 63/58(1)
-undertaking performed more than five years after
date of allotment, 83/29
-undertaking to do work or perform services, 83/26
-valuation in case of public limited company, 83/30,
see 1987/137
-valuation of, 83/30, see 1987/137
consolidation and division of, 63/68
directors, in which, interested or deemed to be,
90B/53-57 & 59 (replacing 63/190)
continued

Shares continued
disclosure of interests in, [see **Directors' interests in shares etc.; Disclosure of interests in shares of public limited company**]
discount, may be issued at, when, 83/27 (63/63 repealed 83/III)
discount, prohibition of allotment at, 83/27
dissenting shareholders of, compulsory acquisition of, 63/204, see 1987/137
expert's report before allotment, non-cash consideration, 83/30, see 1987/137
financial assistance for acquisition of, [see **Financial assistance by company for acquisition of own shares**]
financing by company of purchase of its own, 63/60-AM 82/I, see 90B/155 & 260(1) & 224 & 86/S37(2) & 1989/78
-prohibition of, 63/60-AM 82/I, see 90B/155 & 260(1) & 224 & 1989/78
.exceptions to, 63/60-AM 82/I, see 90B/155 & 260(1) & 224 & 1989/78
.offence in relation to, 63/60-AM 82/I, see 90B/155 & 260(1) & 224 & 1989/78
.power to validate transaction and, 63/60-AM 83/I, see 90B/155 & 260(1) & 224 & 1989/78
.security voidable, 63/60(14), see 90B/155 & 260(1) & 224 & 1989/78
.transaction voidable, 63/60(14), see 90B/155 & 260(1) & 224 & 1989/78
-special resolution for, 63/60(2), see 90B/155 & 260(1) & 224 & 1989/78
.transaction not to be carried out until thirty days after, 63/60(7), see 90B/155 & 260(1) & 224 & 1989/78
-statutory declaration, 63/60-AM 82/I, see 90B/155 & 260(1) & 224 & 1989/78
form of application for, when not to be issued without prospectus, 63/44(3)
interests in shares, Minister's power to require information, 90B/15 [see **Investigations**]
continued

Shares continued
listing particulars, and, 1984/282, see 1991/18
meaning of, 63/2(1)
nature of, 63/79
numbering of, 63/80
offering to the public, meaning of, 63/61-AM 90B/238
paid up, otherwise than in cash, 63/58
-different amounts, on, 63/66
payment for, 83/26
preference, [see **Preference shares**]
premium, issue of, at, 63/62-AM 83/I-AM 90B/231(1), see 90B/207
public limited company, in, minimum payment for, 83/28
purchase by company of own, [see **Purchase by company of its own shares**]
quotation for, 1984/282, see 1991/18
redeemable preference, provisions as to, (63/64-AM 83/I cesser 90B/220)
register of directors' interests in, [see **Directors' interests in shares etc.**]
register of interests in, 90B/80 [see **Register of interests in shares**]
stock, conversion, of into, and reconversion, 63/68
subdivision of, 63/68
subscriber, taken by under memorandum, to be paid in cash (public limited company), 83/35
surrender of, brings allotted share capital below authorised minimum, effect of, 83/19, 83/43, see 90B/256 & 1989/78
transferable, to be, 63/79
transfer of, [see **Transfer of shares**]
transfer of, refusal, notice to transferee, 63/84-AM 82/I
transmission of, [see **Transmission of shares**]
trust held on, [see **Employees' share scheme; Trustee**]
uniform with those already dealt in on stock exchange, prospectus in connection with, 63/44(7)
validation of invalid issue, 90B/227 (replacing 63/89)
warrant to bearer for, 63/88

SHARE WARRANT

bearer of, may be deemed to be a member, 63/118(5)
director's qualification, does not count towards, 63/180(2), see 90B/110
issue of, and effect of, 63/88
offences in connection with, 63/90-AM 82/I
personation of holder of, 63/90-AM 82/I
register of members, particulars to be entered in, on issue of, 63/118

SHIP

charge on, or on share of, requires registration, 63/99-AM 90B/122

SMALL COMPANIES

[see entry under **Accounts**]

SOLICITORS

investigations, duties of, in connection with, 90B/10 (replacing 63/168(6))
privileged communications to, 90B/23 (replacing 63/173), 63/387
prosecutions of officers and members, duties of, in, 63/299(4)-AM 90B/143, see 90B/179
Solicitors Act, 1954, restriction of, 63/397

SOLVENCY

declaration of, on voluntary winding up, 90B/128 (replacing 63/256-AM 82/9)

SPECIAL RESOLUTION

[see **Resolution**]
alteration of
-articles, for, 63/15

continued

Special resolution continued
-of memorandum, with respect to objects, for, 63/10
.with respect to certain other matters, for, 63/28
deed of settlement, for substituting memorandum and articles for, 63/341
director, assignment of office for, confirming, 63/199
-making liability of, unlimited, 63/198
how passed, 63/141
investigation, for, 90B/8 (replacing 63/166)
meaning and provisions as to, 63/141
name, for change of, 63/23
reduction of capital, for, 63/72-AM 90B/231(1), see 90B/260(1) & 1989/78
registration of, and copies of, 63/143-AM 82/5-AM 82/I-AM 83/I
reserve liability for, 63/67
voluntary winding up, for, 63/251
voluntary winding up, sanctioning sale of assets in, for consideration other than cash, 63/260, see 1987/137
winding up by court, for, 63/213

SPECIFIC PERFORMANCE

of contract to take debentures, 63/97

STAGGING, 63/56(5)

STAMP

articles, on, 63/14
contract constituting title of allottee, on particulars of, 63/58(2)
debenture, on re-issue of, 63/95(4)
issue of shares in place of redeemed preference shares, not required on, (63/64(4) cesser 90B/220)
memorandum of association, on, 63/7

STATEMENT IN LIEU OF PROSPECTUS

director, person may not be named in, as, when, 63/179
private company, company ceasing to be, must deliver, to registrar, 63/35-AM 83/I
-delivered by, untrue statements in, 63/35-AM 83/I
-form and contents of, 63/II
public limited company, when required to be delivered by, 63/54
-delivered by, form and contents of, 63/IV, see 90B/221
-contract referred to in, may only be varied subject to approval of statutory meeting, (63/48 repealed 83/I)
-untrue statements in, provisions as to, 63/54(5 & 6)-AM 82/I

STATEMENT OF AFFAIRS

appointment of receiver on, contents and verification of, 63/320
-copies of, 63/319(1)
-when, required to be furnished, 63/319, see 90B/145
creditors' voluntary winding up, in, 63/266(3), see 90B/131
receiver, submitted to, 63/319 & 320, see 90B/145
-contents of, 63/319 & 320, see 90B/145
winding up order or appointment of provisional liquidator, on, 63/224, see 90B/18
-inspection and copies of, 63/224(6), see 90B/18

STATIONERY

examiner, on appointment of, 90/12(4)
directors' names on business letters, 63/196-AM 82/I
foreign company, 63/355
information to be given on business letters and order forms, 1973/163
name of company on, 63/114-AM 82/I-AM 83/I, see 83/56
share capital, if any reference, to be to paid-up capital, 1973/163/9

STATUTORY DECLARATION

company not formed under Act, on registration of, 63/332
incorporation, on, 83/5(5) (63/19(2) repealed 83/I), see 1989/78
public limited company, to accompany application for registration or re-registration, 83/5 & 6, see 1989/78
solvency, of, [see **Declaration of solvency**]
statement of affairs submitted to receiver, verifying, 63/320(4)

STATUTORY MEETING

approval of, necessary to vary contracts referred to in prospectus or statement in lieu of prospectus, (63/48 repealed 83/III)
default as to, ground for winding up, (63/213 repealed 83/III)
-petition for winding up on ground of, only by shareholder, (63/215 repealed 83/III)
.order, court may make on, (63/216(2) repealed 83/III)
meaning of, (63/2(1) repealed 83/III)
provisions as to, and obligation to hold, (63/130 repealed 83/III)

STATUTORY REPORT

default as to, ground for winding up, (63/213 repealed 83/III)
-petition for winding up on ground of, by shareholder only, (63/215 repealed 83/III)
.order court may make on, (63/216(2) repealed 83/III)
meaning of, (63/2(1) repealed 83/III)
provisions as to, and time for sending, (63/130 repealed 83/III)

STOCK

[see **Share capital; Shares**]

continued

Stock continued
annual return to show amount held, 63/125-AM 82/I-AM 90B/244
conversion of shares into, and reconversion, 63/68
register of members to show amount and class held, 63/116

STOCK EXCHANGE

Admissions Directive, 1984/282, see 1991/18
allotment of shares and debentures intended to be listed on, 63/57
company's duty to notify of acquisition by director of listed securities, 90B/65
conditions for admitting shares or debentures to listing, 1984/282, see 1991/18
exemption from obligation to prepare share certificates, 77/2
information to be published by companies on regular basis, 1984/282, see 1991/18
insider dealing on, prohibitions, 90B/108
listing particulars, 1984/282, see 1991/18
flotation of company, and, 1984/282, see 1991/18
"nominee", 77/1(1)
nominee, allotment or transfer to, 77/2
prospectus stating that shares or debentures will be dealt in on, effect of, 63/57
recognised
-meaning of, 63/2(1), 90B/3(1)
-in case of foreign companies, 63/362
-shares or debentures uniform with those already dealt in, 63/44(7)
-when may give certificate of exemption, 63/45
rejection of application for admission to official listing, appeal against, 1984/282, see 1991/18
stock exchange quotation, allotment of shares and, 63/57

STOCK-IN-TRADE

accounts, in, 86/S13 & 15 & 19

SUBSCRIBERS

[see **Members**]
acquisition by company of non-cash asset from, requirement for expert's report (public limited company), 83/32
payment for shares in memorandum, to be in cash (public limited company), 83/35
shares taken in memorandum, 63/6(4), see 90B/253 & 1989/78
signature of memorandum, attested, 63/7

SUBSCRIPTION

company may not give financial assistance for, of shares in itself or its holding company, 63/60, see 90B/155 & 260(1) & 224 & 1989/78

SUBSCRIPTION LISTS

time of opening of, 63/56(1)

SUBSIDIARY

accounts of, 63/150-AM 82/I, see 86/S76 & 90B/41 & 43
accounts, special provisions where company is, 63/VIpII
auditors' powers in relation to, 90B/196
financial year of, to be coincident with that of holding company, 63/153
-when not coincident with that of holding company, 63/152
group accounts required where company has, 63/150, see 90B/41 & 43
holding company of, accounts of, special provisions as to, 63/VIpII
-meetings of, not to vote at, 63/32(6)
-shares of, not to be allotted to or transferred to, or to a nominee for, 63/32(1), see 90B/224
-not to give financial assistance for purchase or subscription shares of, 63/60, see 90B/155 & 260(1) & 224 & 1989/78

continued

Subsidiary continued
meaning of, 63/155
-in provisions as to loans to officers, (63/192(4) cesser 90B/49)
-in provisions as to payments to directors, 63/191(9)
membership of holding company, 63/32, see 90B/224
prospectus, matters to be contained in report to be set out in, when company has, 63/IIIpII
-where issue results in acquisition of, 63/IIIpII
wholly owned, meaning of, 63/150(5)

SURETY OR GUARANTOR

proceedings in respect of fraudulent preference of, 63/287(3)

SURRENDER OF SHARES, 83/43

TABLE A

adoption of, by articles and application of, 63/13
index to, [see **Appendix**]
meaning of, 63/2(1)
Part I of, 63/I
Part II of (applicable to private companies), 63/I
provisions of, as to notice, when applicable, 63/134, see 83/38(6)

TABLE B

memorandum and articles of company limited by shares, form of, 63/16, 63/I

TABLE C

memorandum and articles of company limited by guarantee, not having a share capital, form of, 63/16-AM 82/17, 63/I

TABLE D

memorandum and articles of company limited by guarantee and having a share capital, form of, 63/16, 63/I

TABLE E

memorandum and articles of unlimited company having a share capital, form of, 63/16, 63/I

TABLES

certain former, not affected, 63/3(9)
Minister's powers to alter, 63/395(2)-AM 83/I

TAKEOVERS

automatic deferral of, for three months, 78/3 & 6
compensation for loss of office in, 63/187 & 188
compulsory acquisition procedure, 63/204, see 1987/137
conditions, subject to, 78/11
control of, 78
decision by Minister to refer to Examiner, 78/7
dissenters, minority, right to require company to acquire shares, 63/204, see 1987/137
notification in writing to Minister, 78/5
power of company to acquire shares of dissenting minority, 63/204, see 1987/137
safeguards for shareholders and creditors, 63/204, see 1987/137
service of notice on dissentients, and, 63/204, see 1987/137
-notice set aside if court thinks fit, 63/204, see 1987/137
scheme of arrangement, 63/201-203, see 1987/137
shareholders to be given full particulars, 63/204, see 1987/137
share interests, notification of, 90B/67-79

continued

Takeovers continued
transferee must give dissentients opportunity of selling shares, 63/204, see 1987/137
transferee owning shares in transferor, 63/204(2), see 1987/137

TAX AVOIDANCE

unlimited company and, Finance Act, 1973/67

"TEORANTA"

licence to omit, 63/24-AM 83/I
-public limited company, not granted for, 83/58(1)

THIRD PARTY

proceedings in respect of fraudulent preference, 63/287

TIME

periods of, 90B/4

TITLE OF ACTS

63/1(1), 77/11(1), 82/24(1), 83/1(1), 86/25(1), 90/37(1), 90B/1(1)

TRADEMARK

charge on, requires registration, 63/99

TRANSFER OF SHARES

[see **Transmission of shares**]
certification of, 63/85
deceased member, of, 63/82
delivery of certificate to transferee within two months, 63/86, see 90B/239

continued

Transfer of shares continued
form of, 63/81, ST63-AM 77/8
instrument of, 63/81, ST63
instrument of transfer, to be produced to company, 63/81
manner of transfer, ST63
offences relating to share warrants, 63/90-AM 82/I
power of directors to decline to register, 63/84
refusal to register, notice of, 63/84
registration of transfer, 63/81 & 83
share certificate, evidence of title, 63/87-AM 77/5(1)
shares of company registered under Joint Stock Companies Acts, of, 63/327(1)
share warrant, by delivery of, 63/88
transferor may require company to register, 63/83
voluntary winding up in, void without sanction of liquidator, 63/255
winding up by court in, void, 63/218

TRANSMISSION OF SHARES

bankruptcy, on, 63/81
death, on, 63/81
personal representative, to, 63/81

"TRUE AND FAIR VIEW"

accounts, in, 86/3(1b)

TRUST

notice of, not to be entered on register of members and not receivable by registrar, 63/123

TRUST DEED

for securing debentures, debenture holder may require copy of, 63/92(3), see 90B/105

TRUSTEE

acquisition etc. of securities by, 77/7
debenture holders, for, duty of in connection with compromise or arrangement, 63/202(6), see 1987/137
debenture holders, for, restrictions on exemption from liability of, 63/93
subsidiary as, shares in holding company, 63/32, see 90B/224

TRUSTEE SAVINGS BANK

how may petition to wind up, 63/345(6)

TYPE OF COMPANY

provision for, 63/5

UCITS (UNDERTAKINGS FOR COLLECTIVE INSTRUMENT IN TRANSFERABLE SECURITIES)

[see **Investment Companies (UCITS)**]

ULTRA VIRES RULE

European Communities (Companies) Regulations, 1973, and, 1973/163/6
First EC Companies Directive and, 1973/163/6
restriction of doctrine by statute, 1973/163/6

UNCLAIMED ASSETS

on a winding up, 63/307

UNCLAIMED DIVIDENDS AND BALANCES

to be paid into Companies Liquidation Account, 63/307

UNDERTAKINGS FOR COLLECTIVE INVESTMENT IN TRANSFERABLE SECURITIES (UCITS)

(see European Communities (Undertakings for Collective Investment in Transferable Securities) Regulations,1989, SI No. 78 of 1989)

UNDERWRITING AGREEMENT

prospectus not required to accompany form of application for shares or debentures in connection with invitation to enter into, 63/44(4)

UNDISTRIBUTABLE RESERVES

meaning of, 83/45-51, see 1989/78

UNLIMITED COMPANY

accounts, exception from duty to deliver to registrar, 86/1
articles of association, matters to be stated in, 63/12(1)
-must be registered, 63/11-AM 82/2
conversion into limited company, 83/11, 83/53 (63/20 cesser 83/54)
conversion of limited company into, 83/52
formed and registered under Joint Stock Companies Acts, alteration of capital of, 63/327(2)
limited company, how registered as, 83/11, 83/53, (63/20 cesser 83/54)
meaning of, 63/5(2)
meeting of, length of notice of, 63/133
members of, notice of increase in, 63/12(3)-AM 82/l
memorandum, 63/16
registered under former Acts, application of Act to, 63/326
reserve capital, power to provide for, on registration as limited company, 63/71
share capital, having statutory form of memorandum and articles of, 63/16
winding up by the court of, liability of contributory in, 63/237

UNREGISTERED COMPANY

accounts, 63/377-AM 90B/250, 90B/S (replacing 63/IX), see 1987/137 & 90B/19 & 250
Act, certain provisions of, applicable to, 63/377-AM 90B/250, 90B/S (replacing 63/IX), 90B/243 (replacing 77/6), 90B/250 (replacing 86/21), see 90B/19 & 250 & 1987/137
-when deemed to be company under, 63/349
application of European Communities Act to, (1973/163/8 repealed by 90B/6)
disclosure of transactions involving directors etc., 90B/S
former Acts, provisions of, as to winding up of, not affected, 63/350
meaning of, 63/344
Minister's power to change by order provisions applicable to, 90B/250
provisions as to winding up of, cumulative, 63/349
stay of proceedings against, after presentation of winding up petition, 63/347
-after winding up order, 63/348
Ultra Vires doctrine, restriction by statute applied, (1973/163/8 repealed by 90B/6)
winding up of, 63/345-AM 90B/123
-contributories in, 63/346
-grounds for, 63/345(4 & 5)-AM 90B/123

UNREGISTERED LAND

charge on, registration of, 63/99

VARIATION

[see **Class**]
of rights of shareholders, alteration of certain matters in memorandum not to effect, 63/28-AM 83/I
-application to cancel, 63/78-AM 82/I
rights attached to classes of shares, 63/78

VENDOR

meaning of, in provisions relating to prospectus, 63/IIIpIII/23

VESTING

of company's property in liquidator in winding up by the court, order for, 63/230
of property disclaimed in winding up, order for, 63/290(6)

VOTES

general provisions as to, where none in the articles, 63/134
on a poll, need not all be cast the same way, 63/138
poll, by, 63/137
proxy, and, 63/136-AM 83/I, 63/139
subsidiary not to exercise, at meetings of holding company, 63/32(6), see 90B/224

WINDING UP (ALL MODES) 63/206-211 & 283-312

assets improperly transferred, court may order return, 90B/139
assignment by company for benefit of creditors, void in, 90B/135(2) (replacing 63/286(3))
books and papers, alteration and falsification of, in, 90B/243 (63/294 repealed by 90B/6)
-disposal of, at end of, 63/305
books of account, proper, not kept prior to, 90B/203 (63/296 repealed by 90B/6)
commenced before the operative date, provisions as to, 63/398
contributories in, [see **Contributories**]
court for proceedings, rules as to, 63/312, 90B/235
continued

Winding up (all modes) continued
court power to assess damages against directors' extension of, 90B/148
creditors' meetings, disclosure of creditor connection with proposed liquidator, 90B/147
creditors, restriction of rights as to execution if not complete, 63/291
debts and claims, admissible to proof in, 63/283
-having priority in, [see **Preferential payments**]
disclaimer of onerous property and unprofitable contracts in, 63/290
documents issued by company in, or liquidator, to state company being wound up, 63/303-AM 82/I
execution, or attachment, creditor not entitled to benefit of, after when, 63/291
-goods taken in, duties of sheriff in regard to, in, 63/292
floating charges, certain, invalid in, 90B/136 (replacing 63/288)
fraud, officer guilty of, previous to, 63/295
fraudulent preference, effect of, in, on person fraudulently preferred, 63/287
-invalid in, 90B/135 (replacing 63/286 amended by Second Schedule, Bankruptcy Act, 1988)
-surety or guarantor of, 63/287(3)
-what deemed to be, 90B/135 (replacing 63/286 amended by Second Schedule, Bankruptcy Act, 1988)
fraudulent trading
-civil and criminal liability, 90B/137 & 138 (replacing 63/297-AM 82/I), see 90B/251
-civil liability for, 90B/138
-criminal liability for, 90B/137
-when disclosed in, 90B/137 (replacing 63/297-AM 82/I), see 90B/251
goods taken in execution, effect of order etc. on, 63/292
limited partnership, application to, of provisions for, (63/345(8) repealed by Second Schedule, Bankruptcy Act, 1988)

continued

Winding up (all modes) continued
liquidator, powers and duties etc.,
[see **Liquidator,** various entries]
liquidator
-disqualification for appointment as, 90B/146
-notification of appointment to, 91/133
-penalties for default in making returns, 90B/145
-prior written consent to appointment required, 90B/133
meetings in, court may direct, 63/309
meetings to ascertain wishes of creditors, etc., 63/309
misfeasance proceedings against officer or promoter in, 90B/142 (replacing 63/298), see 90B/251
misfeasance proceedings, extension to directors of holding or subsidiary companies, 90B/148
modes of, 63/206
notification on business letters, orders etc., 63/303-AM 82/I
offences disclosed in, provisions as to inquiry into and prosecution of, 63/299-AM 90B/143, see 90B/179
officers of company, offences by, antecedent to or in course of, 63/293-AM 82/I
proof in, what admissible to, 63/283
-in case of insolvent company, 63/284
property, of company, receiving as a result of an act constituting an offence by officer antecedent to or in course of winding up, 63/293(3)
reckless trading, civil liability for, 90B/138
registrar, information to be given to, when not completed within two years, 63/306-AM 90B/145
related companies
-court may require company to contribute to debts of, 90B/140
-court may order pooling of assets, 90B/141
rules to be made for, 63/312
transitional provisions, 63/398
unclaimed or undistributed assets in, 63/307

WINDING UP (COURT, BY) 63/212-249

alteration of status of members in, void, 63/218
alternative relief to, order for, 63/205, see 90/5(4)
appeal, Rules Or58 r3
application to court, 63/215-AM 83/I
avoidance of attachments, executions, sequestrations, or distress, in, 63/219
avoidance of dispositions and attachments after commencement, 63/218
bank, money due to company in, may be ordered to be paid to, 63/239
books and papers, order for inspection of, in, 63/243, see 90B/251
books and records, no lien over, 90B/125
calls, court may make in, 63/238
commencement of, 63/220
committee of inspection, [see **Committee of inspection**]
-meetings to decide whether to apply for appointment of, 63/232
companies that may be, 63/324-326
company struck off the register, of, 63/311(7)
contributors in, [see **Contributories**]
contributories, settlement of list of, 63/235
costs of, 63/244
court, by, 63/212, 90B/235
court, general powers of, 63/234-248
court having jurisdiction for, 63/212, 90B/235
creditors, and, [see **Creditors**]
debts, inability of company to pay, 63/213
debts, proof of, rules as to, Rules Or74 r103-112
dissolution of company in, 63/249
dividends, rules as to, Rules Or74 r113-117
effect of order, 63/220, 63/239
-dispositions of property, and, 63/218-219
-floating charge, and, 90B/136 (replacing 63/288)
examination of persons in possession of company property, 90B/126 (replacing 63/245)

continued

Winding up (court, by) continued
examination of officers of company and others, in, 90B/126 (replacing 63/245)
fraudulent preference, and, 90B/136 (replacing 63/286), 63/287 [see **Fraudulent preference**]
grounds for, 63/213-AM 83/III-AM 83/I, see 83/12(8)
jurisdiction of High Court, 63/212, 90B/235
"just and equitable", 63/213
leasehold property, and, 63/290
liquidator in, [see **Liquidator (winding up, Court, by)**]
liquidator, appointment, powers and duties etc., on, 63/226 & 229-231
members', reconstruction by voluntary liquidation, and, 63/260, see 1987/137
offences in relation to, 63/293, 90B/243 (replacing 63/294), 63/295, 90B/203 (replacing 63/296)
oppression of member, 63/205, see 90/5(4)
order for, operates in favour of all creditors and contributories, 63/223
-registrar, to be forwarded to, 63/221
-proceedings stayed on, 63/222
petition
-advertisement of, Rules Or74 r11, 12, 14
-affidavits in opposition, Rules Or74 r18
-costs of, Rules Or74 r129(1)
-form of, Rules App.M, Form 2
-notice of intention to appear, and, Rules Or74 r17
-presentation of, Rules Or74 r9
-service, of, Rules Or74 r12
-statutory affidavit, and, Rules Or74 r13, App.M, Forms 6 & 7
-withdrawal of, Rules Or74 r19
petition after investigation of company, 90B/12 (replacing 63/166), 63/205, see 90/5(4)
petition for
-by contributories, 63/215
-by creditors, 63/215, 63/282
-by debenture holders, 63/215 & 282
-by members, 63/215-AM 83/I
-by registrar, 63/215-AM 83/I

continued

Winding up (court, by) continued
-powers of court on hearing of, 63/216-AM 83/III
petition, form of presentation etc., Rules Or74 r8-10, App.M, Forms 2, 3, 4
-stay or restraint of proceedings after presentation of, 63/217
-who may present, 63/215-AM 83/III
petition, hearing of, Rules Or74 r16-19
petition, hearing of, powers of court, 63/216-AM 83/I
petitioner, substitution of, Rules Or74 r19 & 22
proceedings under, Rules Or74 r22
proof of debts in, time may be fixed for, 63/241
property, disposition of, by company in, may be void, 63/218
-may be required to be delivered to liquidator, 63/236
-order vesting, in liquidator, 63/230
prosecution of officers and members, 63/299-AM 90B/143, see 90B/179
provisional liquidator, appointment of, after presentation of petition for, 63/226
rectification of the register of members in, 63/235
requiring attendance of persons before court, 63/224, see 90B/18, Rules Or74 r25(2)
statement of affairs after, Rules, App.M, Form 13
-dispensing with requirements as to, 63/224, see 90B/18
-expenses of, Rules Or74 r26
-filing and verification of, 63/224, see 90B/18
-sent to creditors and contributories, Rules Or74 r29
statement of affairs to be filed in, 63/224, see 90B/18
staying of proceedings, and, 63/222
staying proceedings in, 63/234
-except before Employment Appeals Tribunal, 86/23
surplus, distribution of, in, 63/242
termination of, 63/249, 63/310
transfer of shares in, void, 63/218
transitional provisions, 63/398
trustee savings bank, who may petition for, in case of, 63/345(6)

continued

Winding up (court, by) continued
unregistered company of, [see **Unregistered company**]
voluntary winding up in progress, no bar to creditors' etc. right to petition, 63/282
winding up order, consequences of, 63/221-223

WINDING UP (VOLUNTARY, BOTH KINDS) 63/251-256 & 274-282

alteration of status of member in, void, 63/255
application to court on any matter arising, 63/280
arrangement between company and its creditors in, when binding, 63/279
circumstances for, 63/251-AM 82/I, see 82/16 & 83/12(8) & 16(1c)
commencement of, 63/253
-consequences of, 63/254 & 255
company in, may be wound up by the court, 63/282
costs of, 63/281
declaration of solvency and, 90B/128 (replacing 63/256-AM 82/9)
effect of, on business and status of company, 63/254
liquidator in, [see **Liquidator, winding up, voluntary, both kinds**]
liquidators in, powers and duties of, 63/276, see 90B/131
notice of resolution for, 63/252-AM 82/I, see 82/16
property of company, distribution of, 90B/132 (replacing 63/275)
provisions applicable to every, 63/274-282
resolution for, 63/251, see 83/12(8) & 16(1c)
-advertisement of, 63/252
rights of creditors and contributories on, 63/282
statutory declaration of solvency, 90B/128 (replacing 63/256-AM 82/9)
transfer of shares in, requires liquidator's sanction, 63/255
transitional provisions, 63/398

WINDING UP (VOLUNTARY, CREDITORS) 63/265-273

appointment of liquidator in, 63/267
committee of inspection, appointment of, and provisions applicable to, 63/268
creditors, company to summon meeting of, 63/266-AM 90B/130, see 90B/131
creditors' meeting, 63/266-AM 82/I-AM 90B/130, see 90B/131
directors, powers of, to cease on appointment of liquidator in, 63/269(3)
dissolution of company in, 63/273(4)
final meeting in, 63/273
meaning of, 90B/128(11) (replacing 63/256(7))
meetings of company and creditors, when to be called in, 63/272
provisions of 63/266-273 applicable to, 63/265
provisions as to, 90B/131
sale of company's assets for shares, etc., in another company, when may be made in, 63/271, see 1987/137
remuneration of liquidator, in, 63/269

WINDING UP (VOLUNTARY, MEMBERS) 63/256-264

creditors, meeting of, when to be summoned in, 90B/129 (replacing 63/261)
dissolution of company in, 63/263(4)
final meeting in, 63/263
-when company unable to pay debts in time stated in declaration of solvency, 63/264
meaning of, and how constituted, 90B/128 (replacing 63/256-AM 82/9-AM 82/I)
meetings to be called in, when, 63/262
-where company unable to pay debts in time stated in declaration of solvency, 63/264
members, appointment of liquidator in, [see **Liquidator, winding up, voluntary, members**]
provisions of 63/258-264 applicable to, 63/257

continued

Winding up (voluntary, members) continued
reconstruction by, 63/260, see 1987/137
remuneration of liquidator in, 63/258
sale of company's assets for shares etc. in another company, in, 63/260, see 1987/137
-members dissenting from agreement for, 63/260(3), see 1987/137

WINDING UP, UNREGISTERED COMPANY

[see **Unregistered companies**]

INDEX TO TABLE A, COMPANIES ACT, 1963

As amended by
Companies (Amendment) Act, 1977, s. 5
Companies (Amendment) Act, 1982, s. 21(a)
Companies (Amendment) Act, 1983, First Schedule

PART I

REGULATIONS FOR MANAGEMENT OF A COMPANY LIMITED BY SHARES NOT BEING A PRIVATE COMPANY

ACCOUNTS

accounts, annual, directors shall cause to be prepared, 128
-to be laid before annual general meeting, 128
-to be sent with notice of annual general meeting to members entitled to receive, 129
accounts, proper books of
-directors responsible for keeping, 125
-inspection by directors, open to, at all reasonable times, 126
-inspection by members, directors or company in general meeting may permit, 127
-kept where directors think fit, 126
-required to give true and fair view, 125

AUDIT

auditors to be appointed in accordance with 1963/160-163, 132

BODIES CORPORATE

body corporate may be represented at meetings by person authorised by directors' resolution, 74

BORROWING POWERS

may be exercised by directors, 79
-debt exceeding limit not invalid unless express notice given to lender, 79
-lender not concerned to enquire as to limit, 79
-not to exceed nominal amount of issued capital, 79

CAPITALISATION OF PROFITS

fractions, directors may deal with, 131
reserves, company in general meeting may resolve to capitalise, 130, 130A

DEFINITIONS

"Act", 1
"Directors", 1
"Office", 1
"Register", 1
"Seal", 1
"Secretary", 1
writing, 1

DIRECTORS

director may become director or officer of another company promoted by company, 78
-not accountable for remuneration received from other company unless company directs, 78
expenses properly incurred may be paid, 76
number of, and first, determined in writing by subscribers, 75
remuneration of, determined by general meeting, 76
-accrues from day to day, 76
share qualification may be fixed, 77
-unless fixed, no qualification required, 77

DIRECTORS, DISQUALIFICATION OF

office vacated on, 91

continued

Directors, disqualification of continued
-bankruptcy in State, Northern Ireland or Great Britain, 91
-becoming of unsound mind, 91
-cessation by virtue of 63/180, 91
-conviction of indictable offence, 91
-more than six months absence from directors' meetings, 91
-prohibition under 63/184, 91
-resignation in writing, 91

DIRECTOR, MANAGING

appointment by directors, 110
appointment may be revoked, 110
director, ceasing to be, ends appointment, 110
powers of directors may be conferred on, as defined, 112
-conferral may be revoked or varied, 112
remuneration and terms to be fixed by directors, 110
remuneration decided by directors, 111
rotation, not subject to, 110

DIRECTORS, POWERS AND DUTIES OF

attorney(s) may be appointed by directors, 81
-conditions and period of appointment set by directors, 81
-powers of attorney(s) may be delegated if authorised, 81
contract, director with interest in, shall not vote thereon, 84
-such director not included in quorum, 84
-exceptions for
.arrangement to grant security to director loaning money etc. to company, or for assuming responsibility for debt of company, 84
.undertaking of director to subscribe for or underwrite shares of the company, 84

continued

Directors, powers and duties of continued
.contracts with another company of which director is only officer or shareholder, 84
contract, interest in, must be declared by director at directors' meeting, 83
direction of general meeting subsequent to act of directors does not invalidate act, 80
director, may be counted in quorum at meeting appointing to an office but may not vote on own appointment, 86
director, may hold other office of profit, 85
-remuneration for other office determined by directors, 85
director, may not be auditor, 85
director, professional capacity, other than auditor, may act in for company, 87
-remuneration for professional services, entitled to, 87
directors, minutes to be made of
-appointments of officers, 89
-attendance of directors at meetings of directors and committees, 89
-resolutions and proceedings of meetings of company, directors, and of committees, 89
exercise all powers of company subject to those reserved to general meetings, 80
manage company, 80
pay expenses of promotion, 80
negotiable instruments etc., executed as directors determine, 88
pension, directors may pay to director who has held salaried office, 90
-directors may contribute to fund to provide, 90
seal, official, for use abroad, directors may exercise powers, 82

DIRECTORS, PROCEEDINGS OF

absence of resident from State, may be decided not to give notice, 101

continued

Directors, proceedings of continued
acts of directors or committee of directors valid despite subsequent discovery of defect in appointment of director, 108
chairman, 104
-elected by directors, 104
-period of office may be fixed, 104
-absent after five minutes, directors may choose a chairman for the meeting, 104
committee, 105
-chairman absent after five minutes, may elect a chairman, 106
-decisions by majority vote, 107
.chairman has second or casting vote, 107
-directors may delegate powers to, 105
-may consist of one person, 105
-may elect chairman, 106
-meets and adjourns as thinks proper, 107
-powers to be specified, 105
decisions are by majority vote, 101
directors, meet as they think fit, 101
directors' meeting, quorum, two unless otherwise fixed, 102
equality of votes, chairman has second or casting vote, 101
meeting may be summoned by a director, 101
number below regulations or quorum fixed, remaining directors may meet to appoint new director(s) but for no other purpose, 103
resolution in writing signed by all directors valid as if passed at meeting of directors, 109
secretary required to summon meeting on requisition of director, 101

DIRECTORS, ROTATION OF

annual general meeting, first, all directors retire, 92
annual general meeting, subsequent, one-third of directors retire, 92

continued

Direction, rotation of continued
director may be removed by ordinary resolution of which extended notice has been given, 99
-removal is without prejudice to claim for damages, 99
directors may recommend candidate for election, 96
director, retiring, deemed re-elected unless expressly resolved otherwise, 95
director, retiring, eligible for re-election, 94
directors, number of, may be increased or reduced by ordinary resolution, 97
member may nominate candidate for election, 96
-conditions for valid notice, 96
removed director may be replaced by ordinary resolution, 100
-replacement subject to rotation in place of removed director, 100
retiring directors, those longest in office, 93
-equal service, if not agreed among themselves, decided by lot, 93
vacancy, casual, may be filled by directors, 98
-director so appointed requires re-election at next annual general meeting, 98
-not taken into account for determining rotation, 98
-number of directors not to exceed maximum, 98

DIVIDENDS AND RESERVE

directors may carry forward profits without division, 119
directors may set aside sums as a reserve, 119
dividends
-calls outstanding may be deducted from, 121
-general meeting may direct payment in specie, 122
.directors may deal with fractions, 122
-may be paid to registered address of holder or first holder, to the order thereof, 123
-to be declared and paid proportionate to paid up capital, 120
-shall not bear interest against company, 124
interim dividends may be paid by directors, 117
may be declared by company in general meeting, 116
continued

Dividends and reserve continued
-not to exceed amount recommended by directors, 116
payment of dividend must comply with 1983 Act, 118
shares rank for dividends from date stated in terms of issue, 120

INDEMNITY

assets of company to indemnify director, managing director, agent, auditor, secretary and other officer for liability in proceedings arising from acts in office, where judgement is in favour of person indemnified or such is acquitted, 138

LIEN

extends to dividends on shares where calls not fully paid, 11
on every share where calls not fully paid, 11
share may be declared wholly or partly exempt by directors, 11
shares subject to lien may be sold, 12
-agent may be appointed by directors to transfer shares subject to lien, 13
-demand notice required, 12
-proceeds of sale applied first to payment of outstanding sums, 14
-proceeds of sale, residue, payable to member, 14
-sale may not be made until fourteen days after such notice, 12
-title of purchaser not affected by any irregularity, 13

MEETINGS, GENERAL

annual general meeting
-directors to appoint time and place of, 48
-first need not be held in year of incorporation or year following, 48
-first to be held within eighteen months of incorporation, 48

continued

Meetings, general continued
-notice shall specify that it is, 48
-not more than fifteen months to elapse between each, 48
-other than, called extraordinary general meetings, 49
-to be held in each year, 48
extraordinary general meetings
-directors, absence of quorum, any director or any two members may act to convene, 50
-directors may convene, 50
-general meeting other than annual general meeting, 49
-may be requisitioned under 63/132, 50
State, all general meetings must be held in, 47

MEETINGS, GENERAL, NOTICE OF

annual general meeting, 51
-notice of, 51
notice, accidental omission to give, does not invalidate meeting, 52
notice, requirements as to, 51
special resolution, notice of, 51
ordinary resolution, notice of, 51

MEETINGS, GENERAL, PROCEEDINGS AT

adjournment, demand for poll on, to be taken forthwith, 62
adjournment of general meeting, 58
-adjourned meeting may only deal with unfinished business, 58
-chairman may, with consent of meeting, 58
-meeting may direct, 58
-of more than thirty days requires new notice, 58
-of less than thirty days does not require new notice, 58
annual general meeting, specified business of, 53
-consideration of accounts and reports of directors and auditors, 53
-declaration of dividends, 53

continued

Meetings, general, proceedings at continued
-election of directors, 53
-fixing the remuneration of the auditors, 53
-re-appointment of retiring auditors, 53
chairman, election of, demand for poll on to be taken forthwith, 62
chairman of directors, presides at every general meeting, 56
-absence of, directors present elect a director to preside, 56
-absence of, no director willing to act, members elect a chairman, 57
declaration by chairman and entry in minutes, conclusive evidence of decision, unless poll demanded, 59
-voting not required to be recorded, 59
equality of votes, chairman has second or casting vote, 61
general meeting, resolution decided on show of hands unless poll demanded, 59
poll, chairman to direct manner in which it is to be taken, 60
poll, demand for may be withdrawn, 59
poll demand, other than on election of chairman or adjournment, taken as chairman directs, 62
poll may be demanded by, 59
-chairman, 59
-three members present, 59
-person(s) representing not less than one-tenth of total voting rights or one-tenth of paid up on voting shares, 59
poll, result deemed to be the resolution of the meeting, 60
quorum of three members required, unless otherwise provided, 54
-absence of, at adjourned meeting, within half an hour, members present form quorum, 55
-absence of, within half an hour, 55
.requisitioned meeting dissolved, 55

continued

Meetings, general, proceedings at continued
.other adjourned one week or as the directors determine, 55
special business, 53
-all business at extraordinary general meeting, 53
-all non-specified business at annual general meeting, 53

MEMBERS, VOTES OF

joint holders, vote of first registered voting accepted, 64
member may not vote unless all calls paid, 66
proxy
-form of, 71
-form of, confers authority to demand poll, 72
-form of, must be in writing, signed by member, 69
-must be delivered at address specified not less than forty-eight hours before time of meeting, 70
-need not be member of company, 69
-valid despite death or insanity of member if such not notified to company before meeting, 73
unsound mind, member of, votes by guardian etc., 65
vote, each member or proxy has one on show of hands, 63
-poll, each member or proxy has one for each share, 63
voter, qualification of, objections to, may only be raised at meeting, 67
votes, may be in person or by proxy, 68
votes not disallowed at meeting are valid, 67
votes, objections to, must be made to chairman whose decision is final and conclusive, 67

NOTICES

bankrupt member, to be given to Official Assignee, 135
deceased member, to be given to personal representative(s), 135
general meeting, notice of, to be given to, 136
-auditors, 136
-every member, 136

continued

Notices continued
-no other person, 136
-personal representatives or Official Assignee, if applicable, 136
how given, 133
joint holders, to be sent to first named, 134

SHARE CAPITAL

allotment of shares by directors, subject to provisions of Act, 5
beneficial ownership, company may reasonably require information to be furnished, 7
brokerage, lawful, may be paid, 6
commission
-may be paid, 6
-not to exceed ten per cent, 6
-may be paid in cash or by allotment of shares, 6
discount, allotment at, not permitted, 5
public limited company offering shares to public requires payment of not less than one-quarter on application, 5
share certificate
-to be issued within two months of allotment or transfer, 8
-charge may be made, 8
-company not bound to issue more than one to each member, 8
-to be sealed with seal or official seal, 8
-to specify shares to which it relates and amount paid thereon, 8
-lost or defaced or destroyed, may be replaced, 9
-company may set terms of evidence and indemnity, 9

SHARE CAPITAL, ALTERATION OF

company may by ordinary resolution
-cancel unissued shares, 45
-consolidate into shares of larger amount, 45
-divide into shares of larger amount, 45

continued

Share capital, alternation of continued
-sub-divide existing shares into shares of smaller amount, 45
company may by special resolution reduce, subject to court approval
-capital redemption reserve fund, 46
-share capital, 46
-share premium account, 46

SHARES, CALLS ON

call deemed to be made
-on date specified by terms of issue, 19
-when directors pass resolution, 16
calls in advance may receive interest at rate not exceeding five per cent per annum, 21
-decision to pay lies with directors, 21
-company in general meeting may increase rate, 21
calls may be
-made by directors, 15
-revoked or postponed by directors, 15
call may not exceed one-fourth of nominal value, 15
calls not payable less than one month from date of payment for previous call, 15
calls require fourteen days' notice of time of payment, 15
differentiation may be made by directors on issue between holders as to calls and times of payment, 20
interest may be charged on overdue calls at a rate not exceeding five per cent per annum, 18
interest may be waived by directors, 18
joint holders are jointly and severally liable, 17
payment may be required in instalments, 16

SHARES, CONVERSION INTO STOCK

minimum stock transferable may be fixed by directors, 41

continued

Shares, conversion into stock continued
-minimum not to exceed nominal amount of original shares, 41
regulations applicable to shares apply to stock, 43
"share" includes "stock", 43
"shareholder" includes "stockholder", 43
shares, paid up, may be converted into stock by ordinary resolution, 40
stock, may be reconverted into paid up shares, 40
stock may be transferred in same manner as shares, 41
stock retains same rights as original shares, 42

SHARES, FORFEITURE OF

forfeited shares
-company may execute transfer of, 38
.title of purchaser not void by irregularity, 38
-may be disposed of by directors, 36
-membership ceases in respect of, 37
-previous holder retains liability for outstanding debt unless disposal reimburses company, 37
forfeiture
-may be cancelled by directors before sale, 36
-statutory declaration of director or secretary conclusive evidence of, 38
forfeiture procedures apply in case of failure to pay by fixed date required by terms of issue, 39
member failing to pay call may be served notice of intended forfeiture by directors, 33
-notice to state day not less than fourteen days from date of service for payment, 34
-failure to comply with notice enables forfeiture by resolution of directors, 35

SHARES, TRANSFER OF

member may transfer all or part of shares, 23
notice of refusal to be sent to the transferee within two months of lodgement of transfer, 26

continued

Shares, transfer of continued
registration may be suspended for not more than total of thirty days in each year, 27
registration of probate etc., fee may be charged, 28
transfer instrument must be executed, 22
-transferor remains holder until transfer registered, 22
transfer may be declined by directors, 25
-if fee is requested and not paid, 25
-if share certificate does not accompany transfer, 25
-if it is not in respect of one class only, 25
transfer of share may be declined by directors, 24
- where they do not approve of the transferor, 24
- where share is subject to lien, 24
- where transfer may imperil status of company, 24
- where transfer may imperil tax concession, 24
- where transfer may involve company in additional stamp duty, 24

SHARES, TRANSMISSION OF

bankruptcy, person entitled as a consequence, 30
-directors may require election or registration, 32
-dividend rights unaffected, 32
.but payment may be withheld, 32
-may elect to be registered as holder, 30
.notice of election required, 31
-may nominate another person to be registered as holder, 30
.transfer form required, 31
-meetings, may not attend before registration, 32
-right of directors to decline or suspend transfer not affected, 30
death of member, passes to
-personal representative(s) where sole holder, 29
.only person(s) to be recognised by company, 29
-survivor(s) in joint account, 29
.liability continues to estate, 29
.only person(s) to be recognised by company, 29
death, person entitled as a consequence, 30
-directors may require election or registration, 32

continued

Shares, transmission of continued
-dividend rights unaffected, 32
.but payment may be withheld, 32
-may elect to be registered as holder, 30
.notice of election required, 31
-may nominate another person to be registered as holder, 30
.transfer form required, 31
-meetings, may not attend before registration, 32
-right of directors to decline or suspend transfer not affected, 30

SHARE CAPITAL, VARIATION OF RIGHTS

issue of further shares ranking pari passu with existing shares in class not a variation, 4
shares, company shall not give financial assistance for purchase of own, 10
shares may be issued with such rights as determined, 2
trust shall not be recognised, 7
trust, company not required to recognise, 7
variation of rights in class requires special resolution of class meeting or written resolution signed by holders of three-fourths of shares in class, 3
variation requires ordinary resolution, 2

SEAL

authority of directors required for use, 115
-may be given also by authorised committee, 115
sealing to be signed by director and by secretary or second director or person appointed for the purpose, 115

SECRETARY

appointment by directors, 113
person who is director and secretary may not act in both capacities simultaneously, 114
removal by directors, 113
remuneration and terms decided by directors, 113

WINDING UP

special resolution, may authorise liquidator to distribute in specie, 137
-member not required to accept shares bearing liability, 137

PART II

REGULATIONS FOR THE MANAGEMENT OF A PRIVATE COMPANY LIMITED BY SHARES

alternate director, II/9
-director may appoint, II/9
-entitled
.to notice of directors' meetings, II/9
.to attend and vote at directors' meetings, II/9
-remuneration only from remuneration of appointer, II/9
-appointment in writing given to secretary, II/9
-requires approval by majority of directors, II/9
-appointment may be revoked at any time by appointer or by majority of directors or by company in general meeting, II/9
.revocation by appointer in writing to secretary, II/9
annual general meeting, notice of, II/4
contract, director interested in, may vote thereon, II/7
-may be counted in quorum for meeting, II/7
general meeting, quorum, two members present, II/5
members, number of, excluding employees or former employees, not to exceed fifty, II/2
-joint holders treated as a single member, II/2
Part I applies, with exception of regulations 24, 51, 54, 84 and 86
private company, is, II/2
public, invitation to subscribe for shares or debentures prohibited, II/2

continued

continued
resolution in writing signed by all members valid as if meeting had been held, II/6
-if described as special resolution, deemed to be so, II/6
right to transfer shares is restricted, II/2
shares of other company, directors may exercise voting powers conferred by, II/8
share certificate, to be issued within two months of allotment or transfer, II/10
-charge may be made, II/10
-company not required to issue more than one to each member, II/10
-to be sealed with seal, II/10
-to specify shares to which it relates and amount paid thereon, II/10
share transfer, registration may be refused by directors, II/3
share warrants to bearer, company has no power to issue, II/2
special resolution, meeting to pass, notice of, II/4

SCHEDULE OF FORMS

Abbreviations : D = Director S = Secretary
STDN = Statutory Declaration
P = person interested other than on behalf of company

No.	Section	Title	Signed by
1		replaced by A1	
2	91(3)	Notice of place where register of debenture holders is kept	D or S
3	116(7)	Notice of change in place where register of members is kept	D or S
4		replaced by A1	
5		replaced by B2	
6A	127	Annual Return	D & S
7	91(3)	Notice of change in place where register of debenture holders is kept	D or S
8A		Annual Return continuation sheet	-
9 (B10)	195	Notice of change of directors or secretaries or in their particulars	D or S & new D or S
-		continuation sheet for Form 9	
10		replaced by D4	
11	12(3)	Notice of increase in number of members	D or S
12	256	Declaration of solvency	all or maj. D STDN
13	263	Return of final winding up meeting (members' voluntary)	Liq.

No.	Section	Title	Signed by
13A	273	Return of final winding up meeting (creditors' voluntary)	Liq.
14	263/273	Liquidator's statement of account	Liq.
15	398(1908)	Return of final winding up meeting	Liq.
15A	263	Ditto (members' voluntary)	Liq.
15B	273	Return of creditors' meeting & final winding up meeting	Liq.
16	141	Special resolution	D or S
16A		Ordinary resolution	D or S
17	319/320	Statement of affairs	D or S
18	204	Notice to shareholders	D or S
19	204	Ditto	D or S
21	262/272	Liquidator's account of his acts & dealings & of the conduct of the winding up	Liq.
22	306	Liquidator's affidavit verifying his account	Liq. STDN
23	306	Liquidator's statement of account	Liq.
25		replaced by A1	
28	69	Notice of consolidation, division, or conversion of shares	D or S
39A	278	Notice of appointment of liquidator	Liq.
41		replaced by A1	
42	179(1)	Consent to act as director	D
43	179(4)	List of persons who have consented to be directors	Applt.
44	115(1)	Declaration of compliance	D or S STDN

No.	Section	Title	Signed by
44A	115(2b)	Declaration of compliance	D or S STDN
45	58	Return of allotments	D or S
45A		Continuation sheet for Form 45	D or S
47	99	Particulars of a charge created by a company incorporated in the State	Seal or P
47A	99(8)	Particulars of series of debentures	Seal or P
47B	101	Particulars of charge subject to which property has been acquired by a company incorporated in the State	Seal or P
47C	99(10)	Certificate that charge comprising property outside the State has been presented for registration in the country where property situate	D or S or P
48	99(8)	Further series of debentures	D or S
49	105	Memorandum of satisfaction of mortgage or charge	Seal D & S STDN
49A		Memorandum of release of part of property or undertaking from charge etc.	Seal D & S STDN
52	58(2)	Particulars of a contract relating to shares	D or S
53	107(1)	Notice of appointment of receiver	Rec.
55	35	Statement in lieu of prospectus (private company becoming public)	all D
55A		Ditto (public company)	

No.	Section	Title	Signed by
57	319/321	Receiver's abstract	Rec.
57A	107(2)	Notice of ceasing to act as Receiver	Rec.
58	59	Notice re commission	all D
70	83/6	Application by public limited company to commence business & declaration of particulars	D or S STDN
71	83/9 & 11	Application by private or unlimited company for re-registration as public limited company	D or S
72	83/9 & 11	Declaration of compliance by private or unlimited company with the requirements for re-registration as a public limited company	D or S STDN
73	83/12(3)	Application by an old public limited for re-registration as a public limited company	D or S
74	83/12(5)	Declaration by Director or Secretary on application by an old public limited company for re-registration as a public limited company	D or S STDN
75	83/12(8)	Declaration by old public limited company that it does not meet the requirements for a public limited company	D or S STDN
76	83/14(1)	Application by public limited company for re-registration as a private company	D or S
77	83/17	Application by public limited company for re-registration as another form of company following a court order	D or S

No.	Section	Title	Signed by
78	328,330 332, 83/18	Application by existing joint stock company for registration as a public limited company limited by shares	D or S
79	83/18(4)	Registration of an existing joint stock company, declaration of compliance in connection with registration as a public limited company	D or S STDN
80	83/39(1)	Statement of particulars of rights attached to shares allotted & not otherwise registrable	D or S
81	83/39(3)	Statement of particulars of variation of rights attached to shares & not otherwise registrable	D or S
82	83/39(4)	Notice of assignment of name or new name to any class of shares registrable	D or S
83	83/43(6)	Application by public limited company for re-registration as another form of company following cancellation of shares and diminution of share capital	D or S
84 85 86		replaced by form D6 & continuation	
A1	83/3 83/5 FA1973	Statement of first secretary, and directors & registered office Declaration of compliance Companies capital duty statement	S D Subs. or Agents
B2	113(2)	Notice of change in situation of registered office	D or S

No.	Section	Title	Signed by
B3	116(7)	Notice of place where register of members and/or register of debenture holders is kept	D or S
B4	70	Notice of increase in nominal capital	D or S
D6	52(3)	Members' assent to limited company re-registering as unlimited	all members
	83/52(3)	Declaration by directors as to members' assent to re-registration	all D STDN
		Application by a limited company to be re-registered as unlimited	D or S
G1O	63/23 & 141	Change of Name, Special Resolution	D or S
E24	90/12(1)	Notice of Petition for Appointment of Examiner	Petitioner

FOREIGN COMPANIES

No.	Section	Title	Signed by
1E	352	List of documents presented for filing	authorised person
2E	352	List of directors & secretary	authorised person
3E	352	Return of name(s) and address(es) of person(s) authorised to accept service	authorised person
4E	353	Return of alteration in charter, statutes etc.	authorised person

No.	Section	Title	Signed by
5E	353	Return of alteration in list of directors and secretary	authorised person
6E	353	Return of alteration concerning authorised person or place of business in State	authorised person
7E	354	Return of balance sheet and profit & loss account	authorised person
8E	99/111	Particulars of charge on property in State created by foreign company	authorised person
9E	101/111	Particulars of charge subject to which property in State has been acquired by foreign company	authorised person
10E	112	Particulars of charges created etc. prior to I April 1964	authorised person

REVENUE COMMISSIONERS FORM

No.	Section	Title	Signed by
26	FA1973/69	Companies Capital Duty statement	D or S

SUMMARY OF ORDERS AFFECTING THE COMPANIES ACTS, 1963 TO 1990

SI 1964/41 Companies Act, 1963 (Commencement) Order, 1964

Made 2 March 1964
Appointed 1 April 1964 as the day on which the Companies Act, 1963, came into operation.

SI 1963/42 Companies (Recognition of Countries) Order, 1964

Made 2 March 1964
Recognised Northern Ireland and Great Britain for the purposes of Section 250 (enforcement of winding up order) and Section 367 (prospectus) and prescribed for the purposes of Section 388 (acceptance of published Acts) and Section 389 (acceptance of certificates of incorporation) of the Companies Act, 1963.

SI 1964/43 Companies (Stock Exchange) Order, 1964

Made 2 March 1964
Prescribes the Stock Exchanges at Dublin and Cork for the purposes of Sections 44, 45, 361 and 362 and paragraph 28 of the Sixth Schedule of the Companies Act, 1963. These relate to offers of shares for sale.

SI 1964/44 Companies (Fees) Order, 1964

Made 2 March 1964
Sets out the fees to be charged by the Companies Registration Office.

SI 1964/45 Companies (Forms) Order, 1964

Made 2 March 1964

1. Sets out methods whereby forms and documents in relation to foreign companies may be authenticated.

2. The method of giving notice of acquisition of shares held by dissenting shareholders under section 204.
3. The authentication of registration of charges.
4. The format of the following forms:

52	57a	17
58	47a	57
10	10E	4E
47	44	5E
47C	44a	6E
8E	9A	
47B	9	
9E	18	
53	19	

SI 1973/163 European Communities (Companies) Regulations, 1973

Made 20 June 1973
Gives effect to the Council Directive 68/151/EEC. This deals with the necessity to publish details of documents filed in "Iris Oifigiuil", and notice of appointment of a liquidator. It also requires the filing of an amended copy of the memorandum and articles of association when altered. It modifies the "ultra vires" rule in regard to directors and persons authorised to bind a company. It extends certain requirements of the Companies Act, 1963 to unregistered companies. Rules are also made for company letterheads.

SI 1975/198 Companies (Stock Exchange) Order, 1975

Made 21 August 1975
Prescribes the Stock Exchange in place of the stock exchanges at Dublin and Cork. This arose from a re-organisation of the Exchange.

SI 1976/64 Companies (Fees) Order, 1976

Made 15 March 1976
Amended fees payable under the Companies Act, 1963.

SI 1978/95 Companies (Amendment) Act, 1977 (Commencement) Order, 1978

Made 29 March 1978
Appointed 1 April 1978 as the operative date of the Companies (Amendment) Act, 1977.

SI 1979/122 Companies (Amendment) Act, 1977 (Designation of Stock Exchange Nominee) Regulation, 1979

Made 4 April 1979
Designates Sepon Ltd as a nominee of a stock exchange for the purposes of the Companies (Amendment) Act, 1977.

SI 1980/400 Companies (Fees) Order, 1980

Made 18 December 1980
Amended fees payable under the Companies Act, 1963

SI 1982/255 Companies (Amendment) Act, 1982 (Commencement) Order, 1982

Made 30 July 1982
Appointed 3 August 1982 as the operative date for the Companies (Amendment) Act, 1982

SI 1982/256 Companies (Forms) Order, 1982

Made 30 July 1982
Sets out the format of Forms 9b, replacement Form 9, continuation sheet for both.

SI 1983/259 Companies (Fees) Order, 1983

Made 1 September 1983
Amended certain fees payable under the Companies Act, 1963.

SI 1983/288 Companies (Amendment) Act, 1983 (Commencement) Order, 1983

Made 11 October 1983
Appointed 13 October 1983 as the operative date for the Companies (Amendment) Act, 1983.

SI 1983/289 Companies (Forms) Order, 1983

Made 11 October 1983
Sets out the format of the following forms:

44	72	77	82	86
44A	73	78	83	
41A	74	79	84	
70	75	80	85	
71	76	81	85 (continuation sheet)	

SI 1984/282 European Communities (Stock Exchange) Regulation, 1984

Made 8 November 1984
Imports into domestic law Council Directives 79/279/EEC, 80/390/EEC and 82/121/EEC which deal with admissions to official listing.

SI 1986/257 Companies (Amendment) Act, 1986 (Commencement) Order, 1986

Made 18 July 1986
Appointed 1 August 1986 as the appointed day for the Companies (Amendment) Act, 1986 except Sections 7(1)(a)(ii) and 8(7) & (8). The provision for the publication of accounts applies for each financial year of a company beginning after 31 December 1986.

SI 1987/99 Companies (Fees) Order, 1987

Made 31 March 1987
Sets out revised fees payable under the Companies Act, 1963.

SI 1987/137 European Communities (Mergers and Divisions of Companies) Regulations, 1987

Made 22 May 1987
Implements the Third and Sixth Company Law Directives (Nos. 78/855/EEC and 82/891/EEC) concerning the mergers and divisions of public limited companies.

SI 1987/147 Companies (Forms) Order, 1987

Made 9 June 1987
Sets out the format of the following forms which also replace the previous forms shown in brackets:

A1 (9B, 25, 41A)
B2 (5)
B3 (1)
B4 (10)
D6 and continuation (84, 85, 86)

SI 1988/54 Companies (Amendment) Act, 1982 (Section 13(2)) Order, 1988

Made 29 March 1988
Extends exemption for partnerships of more than twenty persons to partnerships for the purposes of carrying on or promoting the business of thoroughbred horse breeding.

SI 1988/237 Companies (Fees) Order, 1988

Made 22 September 1988
Amended certain fees payable under the Companies Act, 1963

SI 1989/78 European Communities (Undertakings for Collective Investment in Transferable Securities) Regulations, 1989

Made 18 April 1989
Implements Council Directive No. 85/611/EEC on the

coordination of laws, regulations and administrative provisions relating to UCITS (Undertakings for Collective Investment in Transferable Securities). They apply to UCITS whose sole object is the collective investment in transferable securities of capital raised from the public, which operate on the principle of risk spreading and whose units are redeemable at the request of the unit holder. UCITS may be constituted as unit trusts, investment companies with fixed capital, or investment companies with variable capital. The Regulations make the Central Bank of Ireland the competent regulatory body and amend the Companies Acts where appropriate.

SI 1990/224 Companies (Forms) Order, 1990

Made 3 September 1990.
Sets out the format of Form E24.

SI 1990/336 Companies Act, 1990 (Commencement) Order, 1990

Made 24 December 1990.
Appoints 27 December 1990 as commencement day for the following sections of the Companies Act, 1990:

Part I	1-5
Part V	107-121 (all)
Part IX	180 (other than subsections 1g, 2, 3), 181
Part XII	235, 238-240, 242, 244, 245, 247

SI 1990/337 Companies (Stock Exchange Regulations, 1990)

Made 24 December 1990.
Prescribes the Irish Unit of the International Stock Exchange of the United Kingdom and the Republic of Ireland Ltd as a recognised stock exchange.
Revokes Companies (Stock Exchange) Order, 1975 (1975/198)

SI 1991/10 Companies Act, 1990 (Commencement) Order, 1991

Made 22 January 1991.
Appoints 1 February 1991 as commencement day for the following sections of the Companies Act, 1990:

Part II	15, 16, 19-21, 23-24
Part III	25-27, 29-49, 52
Part XII	243
Part XIII	252-262

SI 1991/18 European Communities (Stock Exchange) (Amendment) Regulations, 1991

Made 31 January 1991.
Implements Council Directive 87/345 amending Directive 80/390/EEC co-ordinating the requirements for the drawing up, scrutiny and distribution of the listing particulars to be published for the admission of securities to official stock exchange listing.

COMPANIES ACTS 1963 TO 1990

TABLE OF OFFENCES AND PENALTIES

NOTES:

The financial penalties prescribed in the Companies Act, 1963 have been amended by the First Schedule to Companies (Amendment) Act, 1982.

Summary trial is a trial without jury before a District Justice of summary offences and those indictable offences which may be heard by the District Justice with the consent of the accused and, in certain instances, the agreement of the Director of Public Prosecutions.

Indictable offences are those in which the accused is entitled as of right to a trial by jury.

Abbreviations

AM = Amended by

IN = Inserted by

REP = Repealed by

INDEX TO HEADINGS

	Page
Accounting policies	231
Accounting principles, Departure from	232
Accounts	201, 202, 204
- Books of	201, 253, 254
- Compliance	234
- False statement	234
- Group	202
- Modified	232
- Publication of full or abbreviated	233
- Signing of	203
- Subsidiary	202
Acquisition of PLC shares	242, 243
Allotment, Authority required	226
Allotment of shares	191
- Commissions	191
Annual return	199
- Accounts annexed to	233
- Annexed documents	232
- Documents annexed	199
Annual general meeting	199
Articles of association	188
Auditors	204, 205, 249, 250
Balance sheet, Documents annexed	203
Bankrupts	206
Business letters	209
Capital	
- Alterations in	192
- Increase in	192
- Maintenance of	230
- Reduction of	192
Chamber of Commerce	188
Charges	196
- Register of	194
- On property acquired	194

	Page
Classification	256
Commencement	197
Consideration	228
Court protection	234, 235, 236
Creditors, Meeting of	210, 219
Debentures, Register of	194
Directors	238, 239
- Advertisement of	205
- Disclosure	207, 208
- Disclosure of payments	206
- Disqualified	248, 249
- Of insolvent companies	247, 248
- Prohibition	206
- Register of, and secretaries	208, 209
- Register of shareholdings	206, 207
- Report	204
- Service contracts	240
- Share qualification	205
Directors with unlimited liability	209
Disclosure of interests in shares	240, 241, 242
Documents	255, 256
False statements	224, 255
Financial year	203
Foreign companies	223
Foreign companies, Prospectus	223
Fraudulent trading	218, 236
Insider dealing	245, 246
Investigation	205, 237, 238
Investigation of interests acquired	243, 244
Investment company	230
Judgement mortgages	195
"Limited", Improper use	224
Liquidator	
- Appointment of (All modes)	215
- Disqualfiied person	218

	Page
Members	
- Index of	198
- Register of	198
- Register of, Inspection of	198
Memorandum of association	187, 188
Minute books	201
Minutes	201
Name	197
- Change of	187
Non-cash consideration	
- Experts' reports	227
- Subscribers	228
Oppression	210
Private company	
- Ceasing to be a	188
- Re-registration as	225, 226
Prospectus	189, 190
- Allotment of shares	191
- Statement in Lieu	189, 190
Proxy	200
Public limited company	225, 230
- Misleading name	231
Public limited company, Old	225
- Failure to re-register	226
Purchase of own shares	254, 255
- Financial Assistance	191, 192
Receiver	195, 196, 221, 222
- Abstracts	222
- Bankrupt	221
- Body corporate	221
- Notification	221, 222
- Statement of affairs	222
Receivership, Notice	219
Reconstruction	209, 210
Register of interests in shares	243, 244, 245
Registered office	196
Registers	224

	Page
Resolutions	200
Share Certificates	193
Share Transfer	193
Shareholder, Personation of	193
Shareholders rights, Variation of	193
Shares/debentures, Offer to public	227
Shares, Pre-emption rights	227
Shares with special rights	229, 230
Subsidiary/associated companies	233
Unlimited company, Increase in members	187
Unregistered companies	223, 224
UCITS	256
Winding-up (All modes)	
- Alteration of books	217
- Body corporate as liquidator	218
- Disposal of books,	220
- Dissolution voided	220
- Fraud by officers	217
- Information	220
- Liquidator, Corrupt inducement	218
- Notice	219
- Offences by officers	216, 217
- Periodic returns	247
- Report of offences	246
Winding-up before operative date	225
Winding-up (Court, by)	211, 212
- Annulment or stay	212
- Publication	211
Winding-up, Voluntary (both kinds)	212, 213, 214, 216
- Solvency, Declaration of	
Winding-up, Voluntary Creditors	213, 214, 216, 246

OFFENCE	SECTION	MODE OF TRIAL	MAXIMUM FINE	MAXIMUM PRISON TERM	DAILY DEFAULT FINE	MAX-IMUM DDF
MEMORANDUM OF ASSOCIATION Failure to deliver to the registrar within thirty-six days of amendment a printed copy of the altered memorandum of association; or to give notice of an application to the court in relation to such alteration or to file copy of court order in relation thereto.	63/10(9)	Summary	£250	-	-	-
UNLIMITED COMPANY, INCREASE IN MEMBERS Failure by unlimited company or company limited by guarantee to deliver to the registrar notice of the increase within fifteen days of increase.	63/12(3)	Summary	£250	-	-	-
NAME, CHANGE OF Failure to comply with direction of the Minister to change the company's name.	63/23(2)	Summary	£500	-	-	-

OFFENCE	SECTION	MODE OF TRIAL	MAXIMUM FINE	MAXIMUM PRISON TERM	DAILY DEFAULT FINE	MAX-IMUM DDF
CHAMBER OF COMMERCE Failure to change name in compliance with revocation of licence granted by Minister to use the words "chamber of commerce".	63/24(8)	Summary	£500	-	-	-
MEMORANDUM OF ASSOCIATION Failure to supply copy to any member who requires it.	63/29(1)	Summary	£25	-	-	-
ARTICLES OF ASSOCIATION Failure to supply copy to any member who requires it.	63/29(1)	Summary	£25	-	-	-
MEMORANDUM OF ASSOCIATION Failure to ensure all issued copies contain alterations made to date.	63/30(2)	Summary	£125	-	-	-
PRIVATE COMPANY, CEASING TO BE A Failure to re-register a private company as a public limited company under section 9 of the Companies (Amendment), Act, 1983.	63/35(2) -AM 83/I	Summary	£500	-	-	-

OFFENCE	SECTION	MODE OF TRIAL	MAXIMUM FINE	MAXIMUM PRISON TERM	DAILY DEFAULT FINE	MAX-IMUM DDF
PROSPECTUS, STATEMENT IN LIEU Delivering a statement in lieu of a prospectus to the registrar containing any untrue statement.	63/35(3) -AM 83/I	Summary	£500	6 months, or both	-	-
		Indictment	£2,500	2 years, or both	-	-
PROSPECTUS Failure to comply with the Third Schedule to the Companies Act, 1963 or to issue a form of application for shares except with a prospectus which complies with that Schedule.	63/44	Summary	£500	-	-	-
Issuing a prospectus without obtaining expert's consent to the issue of expert's report with the prospectus or failing to include a statement that consent has been given and not withdrawn.	63/46(1)	Summary	£500	-	-	-
Failure to deliver endorsed copy to the registrar before issue.	63/47(1)	Summary	£500	-	-	-

OFFENCE	SECTION	MODE OF TRIAL	MAXIMUM FINE	MAXIMUM PRISON TERM	DAILY DEFAULT FINE	MAX-IMUM DDF
Inclusion of any untrue statement in issued prospectus.	63/50	Summary	£500	6 months, or both	-	-
PROSPECTUS, STATEMENT IN LIEU OF Failure to deliver to registrar at least three days before the first allotment a statement in lieu of prospectus which complies with the Fourth Schedule to the Companies Act, 1963.	63/53(1)	Summary	£500	-	-	-
Delivery to registrar of statement in lieu of prospectus containing false statement.	63/54(5)	Summary	£500	6 months, or both	-	-
		Indictment	£2,500	2 years, or both	-	-
PROSPECTUS Allotment of shares before the fourth day after which the prospectus is issued or a later date if specified in the prospectus.	63/56 (1 & 2)	Summary	£500	-	-	-

OFFENCE	SECTION	MODE OF TRIAL	MAXIMUM FINE	PRISON TERM	DEFAULT FINE	IMUM DDF
PROSPECTUS, ALLOTMENT OF SHARES Failure to retain subscription moneys in separate bank account pending permission for shares to be dealt with on stock exchange.	63/57(1)	Summary	£500	-	-	-
ALLOTMENT OF SHARES Failure to file return of allotments with registrar within one month after allotment.	63/58	Summary	£500	-	-	-
ALLOTMENT OF SHARES, COMMISSIONS Failure to file with registrar in prescribed form details of authorised commissions paid in connection with the allotment of shares.	63/59	Summary	£500	-	-	-
PURCHASE OF OWN SHARES, FINANCIAL ASSISTANCE Making of statutory declaration by director without reasonable grounds for the opinion as to the company's solvency.	63/60(5)	Summary	£500	6 months, or both	-	-

OFFENCE	SECTION	MODE OF TRIAL	MAXIMUM FINE	MAXIMUM PRISON TERM	DAILY DEFAULT FINE	MAX-IMUM DDF
Giving financial assistance for the purchase of a company's own shares without observing the requirements of section 60 of the Companies Act, 1963.	63/60(15)	Summary	£500	6 months, or both	-	-
		Indictment	£2,500	2 years, or both	-	-
CAPITAL, ALTERATIONS IN Failure to notify registrar within one month of consolidation, division, conversion, subdivision, redemption or cancellation of shares.	63/69(1)	Summary	£250	-	-	-
CAPITAL, INCREASE IN Failure to notify registrar within 15 days of increase in authorised or nominal capital.	63/70(1)	Summary	£250	-	-	-
CAPITAL, REDUCTION OF Wilful concealment by officer of name of creditor entitled to object to reduction of capital or wilful mis-representation of nature or amount of debt or claim by creditor.	63/77	Summary	£500	-	-	-

OFFENCE	SECTION	MODE OF TRIAL	MAXIMUM FINE	MAXIMUM PRISON TERM	DAILY DEFAULT FINE	MAX-IMUM DDF
SHAREHOLDERS' RIGHTS, VARIATION Failure to forward to registrar within twenty-one days copy of court order on application by shareholders to have variation of shareholders' rights cancelled.	63/78(5)	Summary	£250	-	-	-
SHARE TRANSFER Failure to send to transferee, within two months of lodgement of transfer, notice of refusal to register transfer of shares.	63/84(1)	Summary	£250	-	-	-
SHARE CERTIFICATES Failure to provide share/stock certificates within two months of allotment or lodgement of share transfer.	63/86(1)	Summary	£100	-	-	-
SHAREHOLDER, PERSONATION OF False and deceitful personation of owner of share/interest in	63/90	Summary	£500	6 months, or both	-	-

OFFENCE	SECTION	MODE OF TRIAL	MAXIMUM FINE	MAXIMUM PRISON TERM	DAILY DEFAULT FINE	MAX-IMUM DDF
company/share warrant/coupon and obtaining or endeavouring to obtain rights thereto.		Indictment	£2,500	2 years, or both	-	-
DEBENTURES, REGISTER OF						
Failure to keep and maintain register of debenture holders.	63/91 (1 & 2)	Summary	£250	-	-	-
Failure to advise registrar of place where register of debenture holders is kept and any change in that place.	63/91(3)	Summary	£250	-	-	-
Refusal to permit inspection of register of debenture holders or to supply a copy of it.	63/92 (1 & 2)	Summary	£125	-	-	-
CHARGES, REGISTER OF						
Failure to register charges with registrar within twenty-one days after the date of creation.	63/100(1)	Summary	£500	-	-	-
CHARGES ON PROPERTY ACQUIRED						
Failure to register with registrar regis-terable charges existing on property	63/101(1)	Summary	£500	-	-	-

OFFENCE	SECTION	MODE OF TRIAL	MAXIMUM FINE	MAXIMUM PRISON TERM	DAILY DEFAULT FINE	MAX-IMUM DDF
acquired within twenty-one days of completion of acquisition.						
JUDGEMENT MORTGAGES Failure by judgement creditor to obtain and deliver two certified copies of the affidavit to the company within twenty-one days of registration of the judgement as a mortgage.	63/102(1)	Summary	£500	-	-	-
Failure by company to deliver one copy to the registrar within three days of receipt.	63/102(1)	Summary	£500	-	-	-
RECEIVER Failure to give notice of appointment within seven days by a) publication in "Iris Oifigiuil" b) publication in at least one daily newspaper c) delivery of notice in prescribed form to registrar.	63/107(1)	Summary	£500	-	-	-

OFFENCE	SECTION	MODE OF TRIAL	MAXIMUM FINE	MAXIMUM PRISON TERM	DAILY DEFAULT FINE	MAX-IMUM DDF
Failure to deliver notice to registrar on ceasing to act as Receiver.	63/107(2)	Summary	£500	-	-	-
CHARGES Failure to permit inspection at registered office of instruments creating charges.	63/110(1)	Summary	£500	-	-	-
Failure to register with registrar within six months charges etc. created before the operative date (1 April 1964).	63/112(1)	Summary	£500	-	-	-
REGISTERED OFFICE Failure to have a registered office in the State.	63/113(1) -AM 82/4	Summary	£500	-	-	-
Failure to file with registrar within fourteen days notice of change in the situation of the registered office.	63/113(3) -AM 82/4	Summary	£500	-	-	-

OFFENCE	SECTION	MODE OF TRIAL	MAXIMUM FINE	MAXIMUM PRISON TERM	DAILY DEFAULT FINE	MAX-IMUM DDF
NAME						
Failure to paint or affix name of company outside every office or place in which its business is carried on.	63/114 (1)(a)	Summary	£125	-	-	-
Use of seal which does not bear name of company. Issue of business letter, publication, bill of exchange, promissory note, endorsement, cheque, order for money or goods, invoice, receipt or letter of credit which does not bear the company's name.	63/114 (1)(b) & (c), (4)	Summary	£250	-	-	-
COMMENCEMENT						
Commencement of any business or exercise of any borrowing powers by a company which has issued a prospectus to the public to subscribe for its shares which has not observed the necessary conditions in s 115 of the Companies Act, 1963.	63/115	Summary	£500	-	-	-

OFFENCE	SECTION	MODE OF TRIAL	MAXIMUM FINE	MAXIMUM PRISON TERM	DAILY DEFAULT FINE	MAX-IMUM DDF
MEMBERS, REGISTER OF Failure to maintain a register of members in accordance with section 116 of the Companies Act, 1963.	63/116 (1-6)	Summary	£500	-	-	-
Failure to notify registrar within fourteen days of the place where the register is kept and any change in that place.	63/116(7)	Summary	£500	-	-	-
MEMBERS, INDEX OF Failure to index register of members (where more than fifty) unless it is in a form which in itself constitutes an index.	63/117(1)	Summary	£250	-	-	-
MEMBERS, REGISTER OF, INSPECTION OF Failure to permit inspection of register of members or to provide a copy of it.	63/119 (1 & 2)	Summary	£250	-	-	-

OFFENCE	SECTION	MODE OF TRIAL	MAXIMUM FINE	MAXIMUM PRISON TERM	DAILY DEFAULT FINE	MAX-IMUM DDF
ANNUAL RETURN Failure to file annual return made up to fourteen days of the annual general meeting to the registrar within sixty days of the annual general meeting.	63/125(1) 63/126(1) 63/127(1) AM 90B/ 244	Summary	£1,000	-	-	-
ANNUAL RETURN, DOCUMENTS ANNEXED Failure to annex to the annual return certified copy of every balance sheet and report of auditors.	63/128(1) AM 90B/ 244	Summary	£1,000	-	-	-
ANNUAL GENERAL MEETING Failure to hold annual general meeting or to hold meeting in accordance with a direction of the Minister.	63/131 (1 & 3)	Summary	£500	-	-	-
Failure to file copy of resolution to treat a meeting as being the annual general meeting for a previous year with the registrar within fifteen days of its passing.	63/131(5)	Summary	£100	-	-	-

OFFENCE	SECTION	MODE OF TRIAL	MAXIMUM FINE	MAXIMUM PRISON TERM	DAILY DEFAULT FINE	MAX-IMUM DDF
PROXY Failure to include in notice of general meeting statement that a member may appoint a proxy to attend, speak and vote in his/her stead and that the proxy need not be a member.	63/136(3)	Summary	£250	-	-	-
Issue of invitations to appoint as proxy a specified person or persons to some of the members only.	63/136(5)	Summary	£500	-	-	-
RESOLUTIONS Failure to file with registrar copy of resolutions etc. within fifteen days of the passing thereof.	63/143(1)	Summary	£250	-	-	-
Failure to embody or issue resolution with every copy of the articles issued after passing the resolution.	63/143(2)	Summary	£250	-	-	-
Failure to supply a copy to a member who requests it.	63/143	Summary	£5	-	-	-

OFFENCE	SECTION	MODE OF TRIAL	MAXIMUM FINE	MAXIMUM PRISON TERM	DAILY DEFAULT FINE	MAX-IMUM DDF
MINUTES Failure to prepare minutes of general meetings and directors meetings as soon as possible and to enter in books kept for that purpose.	63/145(1)	Summary	£500	-	-	-
MINUTE BOOKS Failure to permit inspection of general meeting minute books by members or to supply a copy thereof.	63/146 (1 & 2)	Summary	£125	-	-	-
ACCOUNTS, BOOKS OF Failure by directors to ensure proper books of account are maintained.	63/147(1) REP	Summary	£1,000	6 months, or both	-	-
	90B/202	Indictment	£10,000	3 years, or both		
ACCOUNTS Failure by director to ensure laying of accounts before annual general meeting.	63/148(1)	Summary	£500	6 months or both	-	-

OFFENCE	SECTION	MODE OF TRIAL	MAXIMUM FINE	MAXIMUM PRISON TERM	DAILY DEFAULT FINE	MAX-IMUM DDF
Failure by director to secure compliance with contents and form requirements.	63/149(7)	Summary	£500	6 months or both	-	-
ACCOUNTS, GROUP Failure to lay group accounts before annual general meeting of holding company where required.	63/150(1)	Summary	£500	6 months or both	-	-
ACCOUNTS, SUBSIDIARY Failure to supply copy of subsidiary accounts when these are not included in the group accounts to any member requesting them within fourteen days of the request.	63/150(3)	Summary	£500	-	-	-
Failure by a private company to supply copy of subsidiary accounts to member of company who requests them within fourteen days of the request.	63/154(2)	Summary	£500	-	-	-

OFFENCE	SECTION	MODE OF TRIAL	MAXIMUM FINE	MAXIMUM PRISON TERM	DAILY DEFAULT FINE	MAX-IMUM DDF
FINANCIAL YEAR Failure to ensure that financial year of holding company and its subsidiaries coincide.	63/153(1)	Summary	£250	-	-	-
ACCOUNTS, SIGNING OF Issue, circulation or publication of balance sheet and profit and loss account which has not been signed by two of the directors (in the case of a banking company by its secretary and three of the directors).	63/156(3)	Summary	£500	-	-	-
BALANCE SHEET, DOCUMENTS ANNEXED Issue, circulation or publication of balance sheet without profit and loss account and auditor's report etc. annexed.	63/157(1)	Summary	£500	-	-	-

OFFENCE	SECTION	MODE OF TRIAL	MAXIMUM FINE	MAXIMUM PRISON TERM	DAILY DEFAULT FINE	MAX-IMUM DDF
DIRECTORS' REPORT						
Failure to prepare and annex to the balance sheet the directors' report dealing with matters required by the Act.	63/158(1)	Summary	£500	6 months, or both	-	-
ACCOUNTS						
Failure to send not less than twenty-one days before the annual general meeting to members and debenture holders copies of the balance sheet and annexed documents required to be laid before the annual general meeting.	63/159(1)	Summary	£250	-	-	-
AUDITORS						
Failure to give notice within one week to the Minister that his power under 63/160(4) has become exercisable.	63/160 -IN 90B/183	Summary	£1,000	-	-	-
Failure to give to the registrar notice within fourteen days of removal of an auditor.	63/160 -IN 90B/183	Summary	£1,000	-	-	-

OFFENCE	SECTION	MODE OF TRIAL	MAXIMUM FINE	MAXIMUM PRISON TERM	DAILY DEFAULT FINE	MAX-IMUM DDF
Acting as an auditor or public auditor when disqualified under section 162.	63/162(8) -AM 82/6	Summary	£500	-	-	-
INVESTIGATION Failure to produce to Inspectors any book or document or refusing to answer any question with respect to the affairs of the company.	63/168(3) -AM 82/7	Summary	£500	6 months, or both	-	-
		Indictment	£5,000	3 years, or both	-	-
DIRECTOR, ADVERTISEMENT OF Delivery to registrar of list of persons consenting to be directors of a company which is the subject of a prospectus or statement in lieu of a prospectus where it contains the name of a person who has not consented.	63/179	Summary	£250	-	-	-
DIRECTORS, SHARE QUALIFICATION Acting as a director of a company without acquiring a share qualification if required to do so by its articles within two weeks of appointment or such shorter time fixed by the articles.	63/180(1)	Summary	£500	-	-	-

OFFENCE	SECTION	MODE OF TRIAL	MAXIMUM FINE	MAXIMUM PRISON TERM	DAILY DEFAULT FINE	MAX-IMUM DDF
BANKRUPT						
Undischarged bankrupt acting as officer, liquidator or examiner or directly or indirectly being involved in the promotion, formation or management of any company without court approval.	63/183 -IN 90B/169	Summary	£1,000	12 months, or both	-	-
		Indictment	£10,000	3 years, or both	-	-
DIRECTORS, PROHIBITION						
Person acting as a director of a company in contravention of a court order.	63/184(5)	Summary	£500	6 months, or both	-	-
		Indictment	£2,500	2 years, or both	-	-
DIRECTORS, DISCLOSURE OF PAYMENTS						
Failure by director to disclose to members payments made to him/her in connection with transfer of shares in company.	63/188(1)	Summary	£125	-	-	-
DIRECTORS, REGISTER OF SHAREHOLDINGS						
Failure to maintain register of directors	63/190(1)	Summary	£500	-	-	-

OFFENCE	SECTION	MODE OF TRIAL	MAXIMUM FINE	MAXIMUM PRISON TERM	DAILY DEFAULT FINE	MAX-IMUM DDF
and secretary's shareholdings in the company and its subsidiary or its parent.	REP 90B/60					
Failure to produce register at commencement of annual general meeting.	63/190(7) REP 90B/60	Summary	£250	-	-	-
Failure to supply copy to member or debenture holder.	63/190(8) REP 90B/60	Summary	£500	-	-	-
DIRECTORS, DISCLOSURE						
Failure by director or secretary to give notice in writing of shareholdings.	63/193(1)	Summary	£500	-	-	-
Failure by director to give notice in writing relating to salaries, payments and loans.	63/193(2)	Summary	£500	-	-	-
Failure by director to make declaration disclosing interest in contracts made by the company.	63/194(6)	Summary	£500	-	-	-

OFFENCE	SECTION	MODE OF TRIAL	MAXIMUM FINE	MAXIMUM PRISON TERM	DAILY DEFAULT FINE	MAX-IMUM DDF
Failure to enter interest in contracts into special book.	63/194(5)	Summary	£500	-	-	-
REGISTER OF DIRECTORS AND SECRETARIES						
Failure to maintain register of directors and secretaries with required details.	63/195 -IN 90B/51	Summary	£1,000	-	£50	-
Failure to notify registrar within fourteen days of change in directors and secretaries or in their particulars.	63/195 -IN 90B/51	Summary	£1,000	-	£50	-
Failure to supply to registrar signed consent of new director or secretary.	63/195 -IN 90B/51	Summary	£1,000	-	£50	-
Refusal to permit inspection of register.	63/195 -IN 90B/51	Summary	£1,000	-	£50	-

OFFENCE	SECTION	MODE OF TRIAL	MAXIMUM FINE	MAXIMUM PRISON TERM	DAILY DEFAULT FINE	MAX-IMUM DDF
Failure by director or secretary to give written notice to company of information required for register.	63/195 -IN 90B/51	Summary Indictment	£1,000 £10,000	- -	- -	-
BUSINESS LETTERS Failure to publish details of directors in all business letters, unless exempted.	63/196	Summary	£125	-	-	-
DIRECTORS WITH UNLIMITED LIABILITY Failure by promoters, directors or secretary to state and to give notice to a director that his/her liability is to be unlimited.	63/197	Summary	£500	-	-	-
RECONSTRUCTION Failure to deliver to registrar copy of court order for compromise or arrangement with creditors.	63/201	Summary	£100	-	-	-

OFFENCE	SECTION	MODE OF TRIAL	MAXIMUM FINE	MAXIMUM PRISON TERM	DAILY DEFAULT FINE	MAX-IMUM DDF
Failure to attach court order for compromise or arrangement with creditors to copies of memorandum of association issued after its making.	63/201	Summary	£100	-	-	-
CREDITORS, MEETING OF						
Failure to supply with notice of meeting of creditors the information required by section 202 of the Companies Act, 1963.	63/202	Summary	£500	-	-	-
Failure of director to give company notice of any matters necessary for such a meeting.	63/202(6)	Summary	£250	-	-	-
Failure to deliver copy of court order for compromise or arrangement with creditors to registrar within twenty-one days of its making.	63/203(3)	Summary	£125	-	-	-
OPPRESSION						
Failure to deliver copy of court order	63/205(5)	Summary	£125	-	-	-

OFFENCE	SECTION	MODE OF TRIAL	MAXIMUM FINE	MAXIMUM PRISON TERM	DAILY DEFAULT FINE	MAX-IMUM DDF
made under section 205 in remedy of oppression to the registrar within twenty-one days of its making.						
WINDING-UP (COURT, BY) Failure to deliver copy of winding-up order to registrar.	63/221(1)	Summary	£125	-	-	-
Failure to file with the court within twenty-one days from the date of the appointment of the liquidator or the making of the winding-up order a statement of affairs verified by affidavit.	63/224(3)	Summary	£500	-	-	-
WINDING-UP (COURT, BY), PUBLICATION Failure by liquidator to publish notice of appointment in "Iris Oifigiuil" within twenty-one days of appointment.	63/227(1)	Summary	£250	-	-	-

OFFENCE	SECTION	MODE OF TRIAL	MAXIMUM FINE	MAXIMUM PRISON TERM	DAILY DEFAULT FINE	MAX-IMUM DDF
WINDING-UP (COURT, BY), ANNULMENT OR STAY Failure to file with registrar copy of court order for the annulment or staying of a winding-up.	63/234(4)	Summary	£125	-	-	-
WINDING-UP (COURT, BY) Failure by liquidator to file with registrar within twenty-one days of its making a copy of court order for dissolution of the company.	63/249(2)	Summary	£250	-	-	
WINDING-UP, VOLUNTARY (BOTH KINDS) Failure to publish within fourteen days in "Iris Oifigiuil" notice of resolution by company for voluntary winding-up.	63/252(1)	Summary	£125	-	-	-
WINDING-UP (COURT, BY) Failure by liquidator to deliver to registrar within twenty-one days office copy of order applying provisions in relation to voluntary winding-up to the winding-up.	63/256 -IN 90B/128	Summary	£1,000	-	-	-

OFFENCE	SECTION	MODE OF TRIAL	MAXIMUM FINE	PRISON TERM	DEFAULT FINE	IMUM DDF
WINDING-UP, VOLUNTARY CREDITORS						
Failure by liquidator to call meeting of creditors when he forms opinion company will be unable to pay its debts.	63/261 -IN 90B/129	Summary Indictment	£1,000 £10,000	- -	- -	- -
WINDING-UP, VOLUNTARY (BOTH KINDS)						
Failure by liquidator to summon a general meeting at the end of the first year from the commencement of the winding-up and of each succeeding year to lay before it an account of his/her acts and dealings and of the conduct of the winding-up and to send a copy of the account to the registrar within seven days of the meeting.	63/262(1) AM 90B/145	Summary Indictment	£1,000 £10,000	- -	£50 £250	- -
Failure by liquidator to hold final general meeting to lay before it an account.	63/263(7)	Summary	£250	-	-	-

OFFENCE	SECTION	MODE OF TRIAL	MAXIMUM FINE	MAXIMUM PRISON TERM	DAILY DEFAULT FINE	MAX-IMUM DDF
Failure by liquidator to send to registrar copy of final account and report of final meeting within seven days of the meeting.	63/263(3)	Summary	£500	-	-	-
Failure by applicant to file with registrar within fourteen days of its making copy of court order deferring the date of dissolution of the company.	63/263(6)	Summary	£25	-	-	-
WINDING-UP, VOLUNTARY CREDITORS						
Failure to summon meeting of creditors in accordance with section 266 of the Companies Act, 1963.	63/266(6)	Summary	£500	-	-	-
Failure by liquidator to summon a general meeting at the end of the first year from the commencement of the winding-up and of each succeeding year to lay before it an account of his/her acts and dealings and of the	63/272(1) AM 90B/145	Summary Indictment	£1,000 £10,000	- -	£50 £250	- -

OFFENCE	SECTION	MODE OF TRIAL	MAXIMUM FINE	PRISON TERM	DEFAULT FINE	IMUM DDF
conduct of the winding-up and to send a copy of the account to the registrar within seven days of the meeting.						
Failure by liquidator to hold final general meeting and meeting of creditors to lay before it an account.	63/273(7)	Summary	£250	-	-	-
Failure by liquidator to send to registrar copy of final account and report of final meetings within seven days of the meetings.	63/273(3)	Summary	£500	-	-	-
Failure by applicant to file with registrar within fourteen days of its making copy of court order deferring the date of dissolution of the company.	63/273(6)	Summary	£250	-	-	-
LIQUIDATOR, APPOINTMENT OF (ALL MODES)						
Failure by liquidator to file notice of appointment with registrar within fourteen days of appointment.	63/278(3)	Summary	£250	-	-	-

OFFENCE	SECTION	MODE OF TRIAL	MAXIMUM FINE	MAXIMUM PRISON TERM	DAILY DEFAULT FINE	MAX-IMUM DDF
WINDING-UP, VOLUNTARY CREDITORS Failure of chairman to notify liquidator in writing of appointment unless liquidator or duly authorised representative is present at meeting making appointment.	63/276A -IN 90B/133	Summary	£1,000	-	-	-
WINDING UP, VOLUNTARY (BOTH KINDS) Failure to file with registrar forthwith copy of court order annulling or staying the winding-up	63/280(3)	Summary	£125	-	-	-
WINDING-UP, OFFENCES BY OFFICERS (ALL MODES) Offences listed in section 293(1) subsections (a) to (l) and (p) of the Companies Act, 1963.	63/293(1)	Summary	£500	6 months, or both	-	-
		Indictment	£2,500	2 years, or both		

OFFENCE	SECTION	MODE OF TRIAL	MAXIMUM FINE	MAXIMUM PRISON TERM	DAILY DEFAULT FINE	MAXIMUM DDF
Offences listed in section 293(1) subsections (m), (n) and (o) of the Companies Act, 1963.	63/293(1)	Indictment	£5,000	*	-	-
			* 5 years penal servitude/2 years imprisonment; or both fine and imprisonment			
WINDING UP, ALTERATION OF BOOKS (ALL MODES)						
Destruction, mutilation, alteration, or falsification of books, papers	63/294	Summary	£500	6 months, or both	-	-
or securities of a company or complicity therein by any officer or contributory of a company.		Indictment	£2,500	2 years, or both	-	-
WINDING-UP, FRAUD BY OFFICERS (ALL MODES)						
Fraud by an officer of a company which is ordered to be wound-up	63/295	Summary	£500	6 months, or both	-	-
or which passes a resolution for voluntary winding-up.		Indictment	£2,500	2 years, or both	-	-
Failure to keep proper books of account in a company which is subsequently	63/296(1) REP	Summary	£1,000	6 months, or both	-	-
wound-up.	90B/6 /N 90B/203	Indictment	£10,000	2 years or both		

OFFENCE	SECTION	MODE OF TRIAL	MAXIMUM FINE	MAXIMUM PRISON TERM	DAILY DEFAULT FINE	MAX-IMUM DDF
FRAUDULENT TRADING Knowingly, or being a party to, carrying on the business of the company with intent to defraud creditors or for any fraudulent purpose.	63/297 -IN 90B/137	Summary Indictment	£1,000 £50,000	12 months, or both 7 years, or both	- -	- -
WINDING-UP, BODY CORPORATE AS LIQUIDATOR (ALL MODES) Body corporate acting as liquidator of a company.	63/300	Summary	£500	-	-	-
LIQUIDATOR, DISQUALIFIED PERSON Disqualified person acting as liquidator.	63/300A IN 90B/146	Summary Indictment	£1,000 £10,000	- -	£50 £250	-
WINDING-UP, LIQUIDATOR, CORRUPT INDUCEMENT (ALL MODES) Giving, offering or agreeing any valuable consideration as inducement for appointment or nomination of self or some other person as liquidator.	63/301	Summary	£500	-	-	-

OFFENCE	SECTION	MODE OF TRIAL	MAXIMUM FINE	MAXIMUM PRISON TERM	DAILY DEFAULT FINE	MAX-IMUM DDF
CREDITORS' MEETING Failure by creditors' representative to disclose to chairman of creditors' meeting connection with proposed liquidator.	63/301A -IN 90B/147	Summary	£1,000	-	-	-
Voting by creditors' representative for himself or for a person with whom he has a connection under 63/301A .	63/301A -IN 90B/147	Summary	£1,000	-	-	-
WINDING UP, NOTICE (ALL MODES) Failure to include statement that company is in liquidation on invoices, orders for goods, or business letters.	63/303(1)	Summary	£250	-	-	-
RECEIVERSHIP, NOTICE Failure to include statement that company is in receivership on invoices, orders for goods, or business letters.	63/317	Summary	£100	-	-	-

MAXIMUM OFFENCE	DAILY SECTION	MAX- MODE OF TRIAL	MAXIMUM FINE	PRISON TERM	DEFAULT FINE	IMUM DDF
WINDING-UP, DISPOSAL OF BOOKS (ALL MODES)						
Failure of liquidator to dispose of books in accordance with . court order . resolution of members in voluntary winding-up . direction of committee of inspection in creditors' winding-up	63/305(1)	Summary	£500	-	-	-
WINDING-UP, INFORMATION (ALL MODES)						
Failure by liquidator where liquidation is not concluded within two years, to send to the registrar particulars about the progress of the liquidation.	63/306(1) AM 90B/145	Summary Indictment	£1,000 £10,000	- -	£50 £250	- -
WINDING-UP, DISSOLUTION VOIDED (ALL MODES)						
Failure of applicant to file with registrar within fourteen days of its making copy of court order declaring dissolution of company void.	63/310(2)	Summary	£25	-	-	-

OFFENCE	SECTION	MODE OF TRIAL	MAXIMUM FINE	MAXIMUM PRISON TERM	DAILY DEFAULT FINE	MAX-IMUM DDF
RECEIVER, BODY CORPORATE Body corporate acting as receiver.	63/314	Summary	£500	-	-	-
RECEIVER Acting as receiver when disqualified by being an undischarged bankrupt; officer of company within twelve months; parent, spouse, brother, sister, or child thereof; partner or employee of officer or servant of company; auditor of company.	63/315 -IN 90B/170	Summary Indictment	£1,000 £5,000	- -	£50 £250	- -
RECEIVER, NOTIFICATION Failure by receiver to . send notice of appointment to company forthwith . send to registrar within two months of receiving it a statement of affairs prepared in accordance with section 320 of the Companies Act, 1963	63/319 (1)	Summary	£500	-	-	-

OFFENCE	SECTION	MODE OF TRIAL	MAXIMUM FINE	MAXIMUM PRISON TERM	DAILY DEFAULT FINE	MAX-IMUM DDF
Failure by receiver to send abstract of receipts and payments to the registrar every six months.	63/319(2) AM 90B/145	Summary Indictment	£1,000 £10,000	- -	£50 £250	- -
RECEIVER, STATEMENT OF AFFAIRS Failure by officers of the company, promoters, employees to prepare and submit the statement of affairs to the receiver within fourteen days of receipt of the notice of the appointment of the receiver.	63/320	Summary	£500	-	-	-
RECEIVER Failure to submit statement of affairs within two months of appointment.	63/320A -IN 90B/173	Summary Indictment	£1,000 £5,000	6 months, or both 3 years, or both	- -	- -
RECEIVER, ABSTRACTS Failure by receiver to deliver to registrar within one month abstract of receipts and payments made up every six months.	63/321(1) AM 90B/145	Summary Indictment	£1,000 £10,000	- -	£50 £250	- -

OFFENCE	SECTION	MODE OF TRIAL	MAXIMUM FINE	MAXIMUM PRISON TERM	DAILY DEFAULT FINE	MAX-IMUM DDF
Failure by receiver to give one month's notice of resignation to holders of floating and fixed charges over the company, the company and the liquidator if any.	63/322C -IN 90B/177	Summary	£1,000	-	-	-
FOREIGN COMPANIES						
Failure to comply with registration requirements in Part XI of Companies Act, 1963.	63/358	Summary	£500	-	-	-
FOREIGN COMPANIES, PROSPECTUS						
Issue, circulation or distribution of prospectus of a foreign company knowingly in contravention of sections 361 to 364 of Companies Act, 1963.	63/365	Summary	£500	6 months, or both	-	-
		Indictment	£2,500	2 years, or both	-	-
UNREGISTERED COMPANIES						
Failure of existing unregistered company to deliver documents to the registrar by 1 October 1964.	63/377(5)	Summary	£500	-	-	-

OFFENCE	SECTION	MODE OF TRIAL	MAXIMUM FINE	MAXIMUM PRISON TERM	DAILY DEFAULT FINE	MAX-IMUM DDF
Failure of new unregistered company to deliver documents within three months of coming into existence.	63/377(6)	Summary	£500	-	-	-
REGISTERS Failure to keep registers in the required manner.	63/378 -AM 77/4	Summary	£250	-	-	-
FALSE STATEMENTS Knowingly making false statements in any return, report, certificate, balance sheet or other document required by the Act and specified in the Tenth Schedule.	63/380	Summary	£500	6 months, or both	-	-
		Indictment	£2,500	3 years, or both	-	-
"LIMITED", IMPROPER USE Improper use of "limited" or "teoranta" by person or persons not incorporated with limited liability.	63/381	Summary	£500	-	-	-

OFFENCE	SECTION	MODE OF TRIAL	MAXIMUM FINE	MAXIMUM PRISON TERM	DAILY DEFAULT FINE	MAX-IMUM DDF
WINDING-UP BEFORE OPERATIVE DATE Failure to deliver to registrar forthwith copy of court order staying proceedings in a winding-up commenced before 1 April 1964.	63/398(2)	Summary	£125	-	-	-
PUBLIC LIMITED COMPANY Commencement of business or exercise of borrowing powers prior to issue of certificate of compliance by registrar.	83/6	Summary	£500	-	-	-
PUBLIC LIMITED COMPANY, OLD Failure by old public limited company to re-register not later than 11 January 1985.	83/13(1)	Summary	£250	-	£25	£500
PRIVATE COMPANY, RE-REGISTRATION AS Failure to give notice to registrar of application to court for cancellation	83/15 (5)(a)	Summary	£250	-	£25	£500

OFFENCE	SECTION	MODE OF TRIAL	MAXIMUM FINE	MAXIMUM PRISON TERM	DAILY DEFAULT FINE	MAX-IMUM DDF
of special resolution for re-registration of a public limited company as a private company.						
Failure to deliver to registrar copy of court order cancelling or confirming special resolution to re-register as private company.	83/15 (5)(b)	Summary	£250	-	£25	£500
OLD PUBLIC LIMITED COMPANY, FAILURE TO RE-REGISTER Failure by old public limited company (which has applied to re-register as another form of company and has not met the requirements) to: (a) meet the requirements; (b) re-register in a form other than that applied for, or (c) wind up voluntarily.	83/16(1)	Summary	£250	-	£25	£500
ALLOTMENT, AUTHORITY REQUIRED Allotment by directors of shares without authority from the company in general meeting or the articles of of association.	83/20(1)	Summary Indictment	£500 £2,500	- -	- -	- -

OFFENCE	SECTION	MODE OF TRIAL	MAXIMUM FINE	MAXIMUM PRISON TERM	DAILY DEFAULT FINE	MAX-IMUM DDF
SHARES/DEBENTURES, OFFER TO PUBLIC Offering to public any shares in or debentures of a private company or allotting shares or debentures with such an intention.	83/21(1)	Summary	£500	-	-	-
SHARES, PRE-EMPTION RIGHTS Knowingly or recklessly permitting inclusion of any matter which is misleading, false or deceptive in a material particular in a director's statement circulated with a special resolution to propose the allotment of shares without applying pre-emption rights.	83/24(6)	Summary	£500	6 months, or both	-	-
		Indictment	£2,500	2 years, or both		
NON-CASH CONSIDERATION, EXPERTS' REPORTS Knowingly or recklessly making a misleading, false or deceptive statement to any expert carrying out a valuation or making a report	83/31(3)	Summary	£500	6 months, or both	-	-
		Indictment	£2,500	2 years, or both		

OFFENCE	SECTION	MODE OF TRIAL	MAXIMUM FINE	MAXIMUM PRISON TERM	DAILY DEFAULT FINE	MAX-IMUM DDF
in respect of non-cash consideration before the allotment of shares.						
NON-CASH CONSIDERATION, SUBSCRIBERS Failure by public limited company to file with registrar copy of ordinary resolution and report required by section 32, Companies (Amendment) Act, 1983 within fifteen days of the passing of the resolution.	83/33(2)	Summary	£250	-	£25	£500
CONSIDERATION Failure to observe the requirements of sections 26 to 30, 32 and 35 of the Companies (Amendment) Act, 1983. 26. Subscription of share capital 27. Prohibition on allotment of shares at a discount	83/36(1)	Summary Indictment	£500 £2,500	- -	- -	- -

OFFENCE	SECTION	MODE OF TRIAL	MAXIMUM MAXIMUM FINE	DAILY PRISON TERM	MAX-DEFAULT FINE	IMUM DDF
28. Payment for allotted shares						
29. Payment of non-cash consideration						
30. Experts' reports on non-cash consideration before allotment of shares.						
32. Experts' reports on non-cash assets acquired from subscribers, etc.						
35. Special provisions as to issue of shares to subscribers.						
SHARES WITH SPECIAL RIGHTS						
Failure to deliver to registrar within one month of allotment of shares with rights not stated in memorandum or articles of association a statement containing particulars of those rights.	83/39(1)	Summary	£250	-	£25	£500
Failure to deliver within one month of allotment statement containing particulars of the variation.	83/39(3)	Summary	£250	-	£25	£500

OFFENCE	SECTION	MODE OF TRIAL	MAXIMUM FINE	MAXIMUM PRISON TERM	DAILY DEFAULT FINE	MAX-IMUM DDF
Failure to deliver notice to the registrar within one month of assignment of name or designation to any class of shares.	83/39(4)	Summary	£250	-	£25	£500
CAPITAL, MAINTENANCE OF Failure by directors to convene extraordinary general meeting to be held not later than eighty-four days of becoming aware that the net assets of the company are half or less of the amount of the company's called-up share capital.	83/40(1)	Summary	£500	6 months, or both	-	-
		Indictment	£2,500	2 years, or both	-	-
PUBLIC LIMITED COMPANY Failure to cancel its own shares acquired by itself or to apply for re-registration as another form of company as required.	83/43(4)	Summary	£250	-	£25	£500
INVESTMENT COMPANY Failure to include expression "investment company" on business letters and order forms.	83/47(9)	Summary	£250	-	-	-

OFFENCE	SECTION	MODE OF TRIAL	MAXIMUM FINE	MAXIMUM PRISON TERM	DAILY DEFAULT FINE	MAX-IMUM DDF
PUBLIC LIMITED COMPANY, MISLEADING NAME						
Carrying on a trade etc. under name including "public limited company" or "cuideachta phoibli theoranta" or abbreviations of those words when not registered as such.	83/57(1)	Summary	£500	-	£50	£1,000
Public limited company carrying on a trade, etc. under a name giving the impression it is a company other than a public limited company.	83/57(2)	Summary	£500	-	£50	£1,000
ACCOUNTING POLICIES						
Failure to maintain the accounting principles in section 5 of the Companies (Amendment) Act, 1986, subject to section 6.	86/22	Summary	£1,000	-	-	-

OFFENCE	SECTION	MODE OF TRIAL	MAXIMUM FINE	MAXIMUM PRISON TERM	DAILY DEFAULT FINE	MAX-IMUM DDF
ACCOUNTING PRINCIPLES, DEPARTURE FROM Failure to state in a note to the accounts any departure from the accounting principles set out in section 5 of the Companies (Amendment) Act, 1986.	86/22	Summary	£1,000	-	-	-
ANNUAL RETURN, ANNEXED DOCUMENTS Failure to annex to the annual return the documents required by section 7 of the Companies (Amendment) Act, 1986.	86/22	Summary	£1,000	-	-	-
ACCOUNTS, MODIFIED Failure to draw up modified accounts for small and medium companies in accordance with sections 10 and 11 of the Companies (Amendment) Act, 1986.	86/22	Summary	£1,000	-	-	-

OFFENCE	SECTION	MODE OF TRIAL	MAXIMUM FINE	MAXIMUM PRISON TERM	DAILY DEFAULT FINE	MAX-IMUM DDF
SUBSIDIARY/ASSOCIATED COMPANIES Failure to provide information about subsidiary and associated companies as required by section 16 of Companies (Amendment) Act, 1986.	86/22	Summary	£1,000	-	-	-
ANNUAL RETURN, ACCOUNTS ANNEXED TO Failure to have accounts annexed to annual return signed in accordance with section 18 of Companies (Amendment) Act, 1986.	86/22	Summary	£1,000	-	-	-
ACCOUNTS, PUBLICATION OF FULL OR ABBREVIATED Failure to publish with full or abbreviated accounts the information required by section 19 of Companies (Amendment) Act, 1986.	86/22	Summary	£1,000	-	-	-

OFFENCE	SECTION	MODE OF TRIAL	MAXIMUM FINE	MAXIMUM PRISON TERM	DAILY DEFAULT FINE	MAX-IMUM DDF
ACCOUNTS, COMPLIANCE Failure by director to take all steps to ensure that accounts comply with sections 3, 4, 13 and 14 and the Schedule of Companies (Amendment) Act, 1986.	86/22	Summary	£1,000	6 months, or both	-	-
ACCOUNTS, FALSE STATEMENT Knowingly and wilfully making a statement false in any material particular in any return, report, certificate, balance sheet or other document required or for the purposes of the Companies (Amendment) Act, 1986.	86/22	Summary	£1,000	6 months, or both	-	-
		Indictment	£2,500	3 years, or both	-	-
COURT PROTECTION Failure by examiner, without reasonable excuse, to deliver within seven days to the registrar an office copy of order permitting disposal of charged property etc.	90/11(7)	Summary	£1,000	-	-	-

OFFENCE	SECTION	MODE OF TRIAL	MAXIMUM FINE	MAXIMUM PRISON TERM	DAILY DEFAULT FINE	MAX-IMUM DDF
Failure by petitioner to deliver notice of petition to registrar within three days of its presentation.	90/12(5)	Summary Indictment	£1,000 £10,000	- -	- -	- -
Failure by examiner to publish notice of his appointment within twenty-one days in "Iris Oifigiuil".	90/12(5)	Summary Indictment	£1,000 £10,000	- -	- -	- -
Failure by examiner to publish notice of his appointment within three days in at least two daily newspapers.	90/12(5)	Summary Indictment	£1,000 £10,000	- -	- -	- -
Failure by examiner to deliver notice of appointment within three days to the registrar.	90/12(5)	Summary Indictment	£1,000 £10,000	- -	- -	- -
Failure to publish statement "under the protection of the court" on invoices, orders or business letters	90/12(5)	Summary Indictment	£1,000 £10,000	- -	- -	- - -
Failure by directors to make, verify by affidavit and submit to examiner within	90/14(3)	Summary Indictment	£1,000 £10,000	- -	- -	- -

OFFENCE	SECTION	MODE OF TRIAL	MAXIMUM FINE	MAXIMUM PRISON TERM	DAILY DEFAULT FINE	MAX-IMUM DDF
seven days of his appointment statement as to the affairs of the company.						
Person acting as examiner who is not qualified to act as liquidator of the company.	90/28(2)	Summary Indictment	£1,000 £10,000	- -	- -	- -
Failure by examiner, or person directed by the court, to publish notice in "Iris Oifigiuil" within fourteen days of delivery to registrar of copy of court order made under 90/17 or 90/24 or of proposal confirmed under 90/24.	90/30(2)	Summary	£1,000	-	-	-
FRAUDULENT TRADING Knowingly or being a party to, carrying on the business of the company with intent to defraud creditors or for any fraudulent purpose.	90/34(1) REP 90B/180	Summary Indictment	£1,000 £50,000	12 months, or both 7 years, or both	- -	- -

OFFENCE	SECTION	MODE OF TRIAL	MAXIMUM FINE	MAXIMUM PRISON TERM	DAILY DEFAULT FINE	MAX-IMUM DDF
INVESTIGATION Failure to give information required or knowingly making statement false in a material particular or recklessly making a statement false in a material particular in relation to the ownership of shares in or debentures of a company.	90B/15	Summary	£1,000	12 months, or both	-	-
		Indictment	£10,000	3 years, or both	-	-
Where Ministerial notice has been given to restrict shares under 90B/16, exercising or purporting to exercise any right to dispose of such shares; or option thereon; or voting in respect of such shares; failing to notify restriction to person entitled to vote in respect of such shares; entering into agreement to sell shares or attached rights.	90B/16	Summary	£1,000	12 months, or both	-	-
		Indictment	£10,000	3 years, or both	-	-
Issuing shares in contravention of restrictions.	90B/16	Summary	£1,000	12 months, or both	-	-
		Indictment	£10,000	3 years, or both	-	-

OFFENCE	SECTION	MODE OF TRIAL	MAXIMUM FINE	MAXIMUM PRISON TERM	DAILY DEFAULT FINE	MAX-IMUM DDF
Failure to comply with Ministerial direction to produce books or documents or provide an explanation or make a statement.	90B/19	Summary	£1,000	12 months, or both	-	-
		Indictment	£10,000	3 years, or both	-	-
Obstruction of exercise of right of entry or search under warrant or right to take possession of any books or documents.	90B/20	Summary	£1,000	12 months, or both	-	-
		Indictment	£10,000	3 years, or both	-	-
Unauthorised publication of any information, book or document.	90B/21	Summary	£1,000	12 months, or both	-	-
		Indictment	£10,000	3 years, or both	-	-
DIRECTORS Dealing in right to call for or to make delivery at specified price, time, and number of relevant shares or debentures.	90B/28	Summary	£1,000	12 months, or both	-	-
		Indictment	£10,000	3 years, or both	-	-

OFFENCE	SECTION	MODE OF TRIAL	MAXIMUM FINE	MAXIMUM PRISON TERM	DAILY DEFAULT FINE	MAX-IMUM DDF
Failure by director to repay surplus business expenses advance within six months of expenditure.	90B/36	Summary	£1,000	12 months, or both		
		Indictment	£10,000	3 years, or both		
Making a prohibited loan to a director or connected person.	90B/40	Summary	£1,000	12 months, or both	-	-
		Indictment	£10,000	3 years, or both	-	-
Procuring a company to make a prohibited loan to a director or connected person.	90B/40	Summary	£1,000	12 months, or both	-	-
		Indictment	£10,000	3 years, or both	-	-
Failure by licensed bank to maintain register of substantial contracts with directors which are excluded from publication by 90B/41(6).	90B/44	Summary	£1,000	12 months, or both	-	-
		Indictment	£10,000	3 years, or both		
Failure by licensed bank to permit inspection of register of substantial contracts with directors.	90B/44	Summary	£1,000	12 months, or both	-	-
		Indictment	£10,000	3 years, or both	-	-

OFFENCE	SECTION	MODE OF TRIAL	MAXIMUM FINE	MAXIMUM PRISON TERM	DAILY DEFAULT FINE	MAX-IMUM DDF
DIRECTORS' SERVICE CONTRACTS Failure to keep copies of directors' service contracts at an appropriate place	90B/50	Summary	£1,000	-	£50	-
DISCLOSURE OF INTERESTS IN SHARES Failure by director, shadow director or secretary to notify company in writing within the proper period of interests in shares and debentures of the company.	90B/53	Summary	£1,000	12 months, or both	-	-
		Indictment	£10,000	3 years, or both	-	-
Failure by director, shadow director, or secretary, without reasonable excuse, to ensure notification by agent of acquisitions or disposals of shares or debentures in the company.	90B/58	Summary	£1,000	12 months, or both	-	-
		Indictment	£10,000	3 years, or both	-	-
Failure to maintain register of directors' interests in shares and debentures.	90B/60	Summary	£1,000	-	-	-

OFFENCE	SECTION	MODE OF TRIAL	MAXIMUM FINE	MAXIMUM PRISON TERM	DAILY DEFAULT FINE	MAX-IMUM DDF
Failure to permit inspection of register of directors' interests.	90B/60	Summary	£1,000	-	-	-
Failure to produce register of directors' interests in shares and debentures at annual general meeting.	90B/60	Summary	£1,000	-	-	-
Failure to maintain register in chronological order	90B/60	Summary	£1,000	-	-	-
Failure to record information within three days of receipt or grant of right.	90B/60	Summary	£1,000	-	-	
Failure to maintain register with index or in index form.	90B/60	Summary	£1,000	-	-	-
Failure to amend index following removal of register entry.	90B/61	Summary Indictment	£1,000 £10,000	- -	- -	- -
Improper deletion of register entry.	90B/62	Summary Indictment	£1,000 £10,000	- -	- -	- -

OFFENCE	SECTION	MODE OF TRIAL	MAXIMUM FINE	MAXIMUM PRISON TERM	DAILY DEFAULT FINE	MAX-IMUM DDF
Failure to restore improper deletion.	90B/62	Summary	£1,000	-	-	-
		Indictment	£10,000	-	-	-
Failure by director, shadow director or secretary to notify company in writing of grant of right to subscribe for shares or debentures of the company to spouse or minor child or the exercise of such right.	90B/64	Summary	£1,000	12 months, or both	-	-
		Indictment	£10,000	3 years, or both	-	-
Failure by company whose shares are dealt in on recognised stock exchange to notify that stock exchange of acquisitions and disposals by director, shadow director, secretary or spouse or minor child thereof.	90B/65	Summary	£1,000	12 months, or both	-	-
		Indictment	£10,000	3 years, or both	-	-
ACQUISITION OF PLC SHARES						
Failure to make disclosure within proper period of acquisition of relevant share capital equal to or exceeding the notifiable level (5 per cent).	90B/79	Summary	£1,000	12 months, or both	-	-
		Indictment	£10,000	3 years, or both	-	-

OFFENCE	SECTION	MODE OF TRIAL	MAXIMUM FINE	MAXIMUM PRISON TERM	DAILY DEFAULT FINE	MAX-IMUM DDF
Failure of persons acting together to acquire interests in public limited company ("concert party") to keep each other informed.	90B/79	Summary	£1,000	12 months, or both	-	-
		Indictment	£10,000	3 years, or both	-	-
Failure of purchaser to ensure immediate notification to purchaser by	90B/79	Summary	£1,000	12 months, or both	-	-
his agent of acquisitions or disposals.	Indictment	£10,000	3 years,	- or both	-	
REGISTER OF INTERESTS IN SHARES						
Failure to maintain register of interests in shares.	90B/80	Summary	£1,000	-	£50	-
INVESTIGATION OF INTERESTS ACQUIRED						
Failure to prepare report of investigation requisitioned by members to investigate purported acquisition of interests in shares in the company and to make the report available at the company's registered office; (and	90B/84	Summary	£1,000	-	-	-
		Indictment	£10,000	-	-	-

OFFENCE	SECTION	MODE OF TRIAL	MAXIMUM FINE	MAXIMUM PRISON TERM	DAILY DEFAULT FINE	MAX-IMUM DDF
where the investigation is not completed within three months, an interim report); and notifying the requisitionists within three days of the report becoming available.						
Failure to comply with court order obtained by company against person failing to give information required in connection with acquisition or disposal of interests in shares in the company which restricts shares under 90B/16.	90B/85	Summary	£1,000	12 months, or both	-	-
		Indictment	£10,000	3 years, or both	-	-
REGISTER OF INTERESTS IN SHARES						
Failure to notify within fifteen days person notified by third party as having interests in the shares of the company.	90B/86	Summary	£1,000	-	-	-
		Indictment	£10,000	-	-	-
Failure to make within fourteen days any necessary alterations in any	90B/86	Summary	£1,000	-	-	-
		Indictment	£10,000	-	-	-

OFFENCE	SECTION	MODE OF TRIAL	MAXIMUM FINE	MAXIMUM PRISON TERM	DAILY DEFAULT FINE	MAX-IMUM DDF
associated index of any removal from the register.						
Making unauthorised deletion from register.	90B/87	Summary	£1,000	-	-	-
		Indictment	£10,000	-	-	-
Failure to restore unauthorised deletion.	90B/87	Summary	£1,000	-	-	-
		Indictment	£10,000	-	-	-
Refusal to permit inspection of register or report made under 90B/84 or to supply a copy thereof.	90B/88	Summary	£1,000	-	-	-
		Indictment	£10,000	-	-	-
INSIDER DEALING						
Unlawfully dealing in securities in contravention of 90B/108.	90B/111	Summary	£1,000	12 months, or both	-	-
		Indictment	£200,000	10 years, or both	-	-
Dealing within twelve months of conviction by person convicted of insider dealing	90B/112	Summary	£1,000	12 months, or both	-	-
		Indictment	£200,000	10 years, or both	-	-

OFFENCE	SECTION	MODE OF TRIAL	MAXIMUM FINE	MAXIMUM PRISON TERM	DAILY DEFAULT FINE	MAX-IMUM DDF
Dealing on behalf of another person with reasonable cause to believe deal would be unlawful under 90B/108.	90B/113	Summary	£1,000	12 months, or both	-	-
		Indictment	£200,000	10 years, or both	-	-
Failure to observe professional secrecy.	90B/118	Summary	£1,000	12 months, or both	-	-
		Indictment	£10,000	3 years, or both		
WINDING-UP, VOLUNTARY CREDITORS						
Failure by liquidator to comply with 90B/131.	90B/131	Summary	£1,000	12 months, or both	-	-
		Indictment	£10,000	3 years, or both	-	-
WINDING-UP, REPORT OF OFFENCES						
Failure by liquidator or receiver to include in periodic returns a report relating to any past or present officer or member of the company who is the subject of a disqualification order or who	90B/144	Summary	£1,000	-	-	-
		Indictment	£10,000	-	-	-

OFFENCE	SECTION	MODE OF TRIAL	MAXIMUM FINE	MAXIMUM PRISON TERM	DAILY DEFAULT FINE	MAX-IMUM DDF
has been made personally responsible for debts of a company.						
WINDING-UP, PERIODIC RETURNS						
Failure by liquidator or receiver to make any returns required by the Companies Acts.	90B/145	Summary Indictment	£1,000 £10,000	- -	£50 £250	- -
DIRECTORS OF INSOLVENT COMPANIES						
Failure by liquidator within seven days of the relevant date to notify every director that they are persons to whom 90B/149-158 applies and to notify the registrar of the name of every such person.	90B/151	Summary Indictment	£1,000 £10,000	- -	£50 £250	- -
Failure of liquidator to notify court of his opinion that the interests of any other company or its creditors may be placed in jeopardy because a director of the insolvent company is acting as a director	90B/151	Summary Indictment	£1,000 £10,000	- -	£50 £250	- -

OFFENCE	SECTION	MODE OF TRIAL	MAXIMUM FINE	MAXIMUM PRISON TERM	DAILY DEFAULT FINE	MAX-IMUM DDF
or is involved in the promotion or formation of such other company.						
Failure by liquidator to notify creditors and contributories of receipt of notice of intention of director of insolvent company to apply to court for relief from 90B/150.	90B/152	Summary	£1,000	-	-	-
		Indictment	£10,000	-	-	-
DISQUALIFIED DIRECTOR Person acting in contravention of disqualification order.	90B/161	Summary	£1,000	12 months, or both	-	-
		Indictment	£10,000	3 years, or both	-	-
Failure by liquidator to report to court where disqualified person is or becomes a director of a company which commences to be wound up (and is unable to pay its debts) within five years of the date of commencement of the winding-up of the company whose insolvency caused his disqualification.	90B/161	Summary	£1,000	-	-	-

OFFENCE	SECTION	MODE OF TRIAL	MAXIMUM FINE	MAXIMUM PRISON TERM	DAILY DEFAULT FINE	MAX-IMUM DDF
Director or other officer or member of committee of management or trustee of any company knowingly acting in accordance with the directions or instructions of a disqualified person.	90B/164	Summary	£1,000	12 months, or both	-	-
		Indictment	£10,000	3 years, or both	-	-
Failure by director or shadow director charged with alleged fraud or dishonesty to give written advance notice to the court of required particulars of directorships.	90B/166	Summary	£1,000	12 months, or both	-	-
		Indictment	£10,000	3 years, or both	-	-
AUDITORS						
Failure by auditor to notify registrar of companies within fourteen days of service of notice of resignation on company.	90B/185	Summary	£1,000	12 months, or both	-	-
		Indictment	£10,000	3 years, or both	-	-
Failure by auditor to include required material in notice of resignation.	90B/185	Summary	£1,000	12 months, or both	-	-
		Indictment	£10,000	3 years, or both	-	-

OFFENCE	SECTION	MODE OF TRIAL	MAXIMUM FINE	MAXIMUM PRISON TERM	DAILY DEFAULT FINE	MAX-IMUM DDF
Failure to give, within fourteen days, notice to persons entitled to receive documents under 63/159(1) of an auditor's written notice of intention to resign in which are set out the circumstances connected with the resignation which should be brought to the notice of the members or creditors of the company.	90B/185	Summary	£1,000	12 months, or both	-	-
		Indictment	£10,000	3 years, or both	-	-
Failure to convene a general meeting within fourteen days of service of notice by auditor for the purpose of receiving and considering an account and explanation of the circumstances connected with the auditor's resignation.	90B/186	Summary	£1,000	12 months, or both	-	-
		Indictment	£10,000	3 years, or both	-	-
Failure to send to persons entitled to receive documents under 63/159(1) and to the registrar a copy of any further statement by auditor to members.	90B/186	Summary	£1,000	12 months, or both	-	-
		Indictment	£10,000	3 years, or both	-	-

OFFENCE	SECTION	MODE OF TRIAL	MAXIMUM FINE	MAXIMUM PRISON TERM	DAILY DEFAULT FINE	MAX-IMUM DDF
Failure to send to the auditor notices of the meeting and all other documents relating thereto and to permit him to attend and be heard on any part of the business which concerns him as former auditor.	90B/186	Summary	£1,000	12 months, or both	-	-
		Indictment	£10,000	3 years, or both	-	-
Disqualified person acting as auditor or public auditor.	90B/187	Summary	£1,000	-	£50	-
		Indictment	£5,000	-	£100	-
Failure to vacate office as auditor or public auditor on becoming disqualified and to give written notice of this to the company, society or friendly society.	90B/187	Summary	£1,000	-	£50	-
		Indictment	£5,000	-	£100	-
Failure by auditor to serve notice on company and to notify registrar within seven days of such notice of his opinion that company is contravening or has contravened requirement to maintain proper books of account.	90B/194	Summary	£1,000	12 months, or both	-	-
		Indictment	£10,000	3 years, or both	-	-

OFFENCE	SECTION	MODE OF TRIAL	MAXIMUM FINE	MAXIMUM PRISON TERM	DAILY DEFAULT FINE	MAX-IMUM DDF
Person who is subject of disqualification order becoming or remaining partner in firm of auditors; giving directions or instructions in relation to conduct of audit; working in any capacity in conduct of audit of accounts of a company.	90B/195	Summary	£1,000	12 months, or both	-	-
		Indictment	£10,000	3 years, or both	-	-
Failure by subsidiary company or its auditor to give to the auditors of the holding company such information and explanations as may be required.	90B/196	Summary	£1,000	12 months, or both	-	-
		Indictment	£10,000	3 years, or both	-	-
Failure of holding company to obtain from its subsidiary information needed for purposes of audit.	90B/196	Summary	£1,000	12 months, or both	-	-
		Indictment	£10,000	3 years, or both	-	-
Knowingly or recklessly making a statement to the auditor, when an officer or employee of the company, which is misleading or false or deceptive in a material particular.	90B/197	Summary	£1,000	12 months, or both	-	-
		Indictment	£10,000	3 years, or both	-	-

OFFENCE	SECTION	MODE OF TRIAL	MAXIMUM FINE	MAXIMUM PRISON TERM	DAILY DEFAULT FINE	MAX-IMUM DDF
Failure to provide to auditor within two days of requisition any information or explanations required.	90B/197	Summary	£1,000	12 months, or both	-	-
		Indictment	£10,000	3 years, or both	-	-
Failure by recognised body of accountants to deliver within one month of renewal/recognition to the registrar of companies list of members qualified for appointment as auditors.	90B/199	Summary	£1,000	12 months, or both	-	-
		Indictment	£10,000	3 years, or both		
Failure by recognised body of accountants to deliver within one month of their qualification list of members qualified for appointment as auditors.	90B/200	Summary	£1,000	12 months, or both	-	-
		Indictment	£10,000	3 years, or both	-	-
BOOKS OF ACCOUNT Failure to keep, on a continuous and consistent basis, proper books of account.	90B/202	Summary	£1,000	12 months, or both	-	-
		Indictment	£10,000	3 years, or both	-	-

OFFENCE	SECTION	MODE OF TRIAL	MAXIMUM FINE	MAXIMUM PRISON TERM	DAILY DEFAULT FINE	MAX-IMUM DDF
Failure to keep proper books of account being considered to have contributed to a company's insolvency.	90B/203	Summary	£1,000	6 months, or both	-	-
		Indictment	£10,000	5 years, or both	-	-
PURCHASE OF OWN SHARES Failure to retain and permit inspection of contracts for purchases of own shares.	90B/222	Summary	£1,000	12 months, or both	-	-
		Indictment	£10,000	3 years, or both	-	-
Failure to deliver to registrar within twenty-eight days return relating to purchase of own shares.	90B/226	Summary	£1,000	12 months, or both	-	-
		Indictment	£10,000	3 years, or both	-	-
Failure to comply with Ministerial regulations relating to purchase of own shares.	90B/228	Summary	£1,000	12 months, or both	-	-
		Indictment	£10,000	3 years, or both	-	-

OFFENCE	SECTION	MODE OF TRIAL	MAXIMUM FINE	MAXIMUM PRISON TERM	DAILY DEFAULT FINE	MAX-IMUM DDF
Failure by quoted company to notify recognised stock exchange.	90B/229	Summary	£1,000	12 months, or both	-	-
		Indictment	£10,000	3 years, or both	-	-
Contravention of procedures set out in 90B/208-211, 218, 222-224.	90B/234	Summary	£1,000	12 months, or both	-	-
		Indictment	£10,000	3 years, or both	-	-
FALSE INFORMATION						
Furnishing false information in purported compliance of the Companies Acts.	90B/242	Summary	£1,000	12 months, or both	-	-
		Indictment	£10,000	3 years, or both (7 years)	-	-
(In certain circumstances prison term may be increased)						
DOCUMENTS						
Destroying, mutilating or falsifying any book or document or being privy thereto.	90B/243	Summary	£1,000	12 months, or both	-	-
		Indictment	£10,000	3 years, or both	-	-

OFFENCE	SECTION	MODE OF TRIAL	MAXIMUM FINE	MAXIMUM PRISON TERM	DAILY DEFAULT FINE	MAX-IMUM DDF
Fraudulently parting with, altering or making an omission in any book or document or being privy thereto.	90B/243	Summary	£1,000	12 months, or both	-	-
		Indictment	£10,000	3 years, or both	-	-
CLASSIFICATION Failing to comply with any system of classification required by Ministerial regulation for documents to be filed with the registrar.	90B/247	Summary	£1,000	-	-	-
		Indictment	£10,000	-	-	-
UCITS Contravention of 90B/252-261; any regulation made thereon; or any condition laid down under 90B/257 by Central Bank of Ireland.	90B/262	Summary	£1,000	12 months, or both	-	-
		Indictment	£10,000	3 years, or both	-	-